ENGLISH PHRASAL VERBS THROUGH STORIES

200 phrasal verbs and 150 idioms and phrases through engaging stories

Daniela Casti

Downloadable Audio

Go to **https://jumpshare.com/b/4kOY3SOwC0kt4WERSntA** to download the audio files for the listening activities to your computer or device.

ISBN: 979-8-218-68630-7

Proof-reading: D.Casti, T. Mallinson, J. Poulton (for the stories)
Audio recording: T. Mallinson, D. Casti
Audio editing: D. Casti
Book Cover and Interior Design: Walton Burns, Alphabet Publishing
Country of Manufacture Specified on Last Page
First Printing 2025

TABLE OF CONTENTS

HOW TO USE THIS BOOK

English Phrasal Verbs through Stories is an activity book meant both for self-study and for classroom use. It is comprised of 15 chapters, each presenting a specific set of phrasal verbs through the context provided by a story. What makes my approach different is that each story (Text 1) comes with a parallel explanatory text (Text 2) written very similarly to the original one (Text 1). The purpose is to supply both the phrasal verb and its equivalent (e.g. put out the fire vs extinguish the fire) so that the student can compare the versions line by line and infer the meaning of the phrasal verbs and idiomatic expressions proposed in the first text. Each phrasal verb is underlined only once, even if it may appear other times in the story. Starting from Chapter 5, the level of difficulty gradually increases, and the student should notice that Text 1, which contains phrasal verbs and idiomatic expressions, is meant to be more informal, while Text 2 is meant to be a little more formal (e.g. ask vs inquire; doesn't vs does not).

The book presents both phrasal verbs and idiomatic expressions which are widely used both in American English (AmE) and British English (BrE), unless explicitly specified. The author used American English (AmE) spelling and vocabulary. If the student is more familiar with British English (BrE) spelling or vocabulary, an appendix at the end of the book is provided with the differences between American English (AmE) and British English (BrE).

Each chapter is organized in the exact same way. The student first reads and listens to the text containing the phrasal verbs (Text 1) and follows along from the second text (Text 2), so as to notice the patterns on their own. This is supposed to awaken a process of self-discovery in the student. After that, the student listens to the second text (Text 2) and follows along from the first text (Text 1), so as to confirm their first impressions. As a third step, the student will listen to and possibly repeat the first text (Text 1) sentence by sentence. Subsequently, they will complete the vocabulary section finding the meaning of each language item by comparing Text 1 and Text 2. It is advisable to always check the solutions and the glossary at the end of the book for a more complete definition. A series of fill-in-the blank strategy based activities, aimed at facilitating the student's understanding and recall, ensues.

The book is intended for intermediate (B1+, B2) and upper-intermediate (B2+) ESL, EFL adults and young adults who may possibly need to sit a language exam, or approach the topic of phrasal verbs and idiomatic expressions in a different way. Some advanced students (C1) may also find the book useful.

To the Student

Dear Student,

Are phrasal verbs good or bad? Native speakers love them and use them all the time. Non-native speakers, especially those from Latin-based languages, find it hard to understand the need of using two (or more) words instead of one to express a concept.

Why do we need to say: "Quick! Put out the fire!" And not simply "Quick! Extinguish the fire!"? Partially it's due to imitation. As a social individual, you want to be understood. In a situation of emergency, no native speaker would say "Quick! Extinguish the fire!" because it sounds too formal, and it's probably not strong enough to convey all the stress involved in trying to stop the flames.

So, are phrasal verbs good of bad? My answer is: neutral. Some phrasal verbs are taught to us at an early stage, we take them in and don't question it. We learn that "I get up at 6:00 am" means that at that time I leave my bed. We don't even think that there could be another way of saying it. We accept it in our system and go on with the rest.

As we progress in our learning, we come across phrasal verbs and continue to absorb them without putting much thought into it. It's only when we are finally explicitly presented the topic that we sort of "panic" and feel overwhelmed.

"English Phrasal Verbs through Stories" is an attempt to introduce phrasal verbs in an organized but engaging way. As a non-native speaker myself, I found the idea of grouping them under the category of a common main verb "Be","Carry" etc. somehow comforting.

At the same time, a strategy needed to be found in order to manage the myriad of particles associated with the same verb, and propose it in a way that would create clarity.

That's why I thought about stories with parallel texts. When I started learning English, I very fondly remember reading side-by-side novels (English/Italian). I found it an excellent way to explore this wonderful language on my own and have the support of my mother tongue in case of necessity.

Side by side texts encourage the "noticing" process in the student, awakening curiosity and autonomy because the teacher isn't needed. When a learner "notices" a language item, they are more likely to remember it.

Parallel texts also provide language in context, which may trigger a number of association of ideas, or inner images that make them more likely to sink into the learner's mind.

Finally, stories are entertaining. We all remember things better when we become interested, even better if absorbed, in something.

Despite the main focus of the chapters being phrasal verbs, a number of idioms and phrases is also proposed in the book. Why? Because idioms and phrases are a natural element of any language. Learning and using them helps the student to connect more rapidly both with English native speakers and with their own identity, especially when there are similarities between the idioms in English and the ones in their own mother tongue.

Please, be patient with yourself and remember that you are doing great. You deserve respect just for the simple fact that you are embarking on a new journey: learning something new. I hope you will find this method enjoyable and useful, and that by the end of the book you will be able to say: "Phrasal verbs are a breeze!" ("Phrasal verbs are easy!").

Best wishes,

Daniela Casti

Phrasal Verb Types

Phrasal verbs are verbs that consist of a verb and a particle. A particle can be a preposition or an adverb. The meaning of a phrasal verb cannot be interpreted literally. The union of the verb and the particle create a new meaning.

Ex. To put off a meeting = to postpone a meeting

There are four main types of phrasal verbs:

➡ **TYPE 1: Intransitive inseparable**

Verb and particle are not followed by an object.

Ex. The plane took off.
   Jack and his girlfriend have broken up.

➡ **TYPE 2: Transitive separable**

Verb and particle are followed by an object and can be separable.

Ex. She put on her shoes.
   She put her shoes on.

Ex. Turn on the lights, please.
   Turn the lights on, please.

NOTE:

If we replace the object with an object pronoun, this always goes between the verb and the preposition (or particle).

Ex. She put them on. → NOT She put on them
   Turn them on, please. → NOT Turn on them, please.

➡ **TYPE 3: Transitive inseparable**

Verb and particle are followed by an object but they cannot be separated.

Ex. She is going to look after my cat while I'm on my business trip.

NOT —-> ~~She's going to look my cat after.~~

Ex. He came across an old schoolmate of his.

NOT → ~~He came an old schoolmate of his across.~~

➡️ **TYPE 4: Transitive inseparable with two prepositions**

The verb is followed by two prepositions and by an object and they cannot be separated.

Ex. We ran out of milk.

NOT → ~~We ran milk out of.~~

Ex. She came up with an idea.

NOT → ~~She came with an idea up.~~

➡️ **Each phrasal verb can have different meanings and belong to different types.**

Ex. Take off (Type 1 — Intransitive inseparable)

The plane took off at 7:00 am on time.

Ex. Take (sth) off (Type 2 — Transitive separable)

I took off my shoes.

CHAPTER 1: BE — AN UNEXPECTED OPPORTUNITY

Text 1 🎧1

The Bradley Family were a very well off family. They had a mansion in the Hamptons with a guest house and a swimming pool for their summer vacations. When the summer was over, they spent their winter months in a penthouse in Manhattan. They were looking for a house-sitter to take on: a person who could look after the house all year round, but especially while the family was away. In principle, they were generally off from August until May, but sometimes they might be back for Easter or even Christmas. All they needed was somebody who would be in all the time, and would be up in case they arrived during the night. Most importantly, they needed somebody who would be there in case any criminal might be up to no good on their property. They offered the job to John: he could go live there with his family for $100,000 a year. Now, it was up to John to decide whether to take on the job or not. What would you do if you were in John's shoes?

Text 2 🎧2

The Bradley Family were a very wealthy family. They owned a mansion in the Hamptons with a guest house and a swimming pool for their summer vacations. When the summer ended, they spent their winter months in a penthouse in Manhattan. They were searching for a house-sitter to hire: a person who could attend to the house all year round while the family was absent. In principle, they generally left from August until May, but sometimes they might return for Easter or even Christmas. All they needed was somebody who would be home all the time, and would be awake in case they arrived during the night. Most importantly, they needed somebody who would be there in case any criminal might violate the law on their property. They offered the job to John: he could go live there with his family for $100,000 a year. Now, John had to decide whether to accept the job or not. What would you do if you were John?

Vocabulary:

Be well off (phrase) = _____

Be over (phrasal verb) = _____

Look for (phrasal verb) = _____

Take (sb) on (phrasal verb) = _____

Look after (phrasal verb) = _____

Be away (phrasal verb) = _____

Be off (phrasal verb) = _____

Be back (phrasal verb) = _____

Be in (phrasal verb) = _____

Be up (phrasal verb) = _____

Be up to (sth) (phrasal verb) = _____

Be up to (sb) (phrasal verb) = _____

Take (sth) on (phrasal verb) = _____

Be in sb's shoes (idiom) = _____

Exercise 1.1 🎧 1

Listen to text n. 1 while following along from text 2.

Exercise 1.2 🎧 2

Listen to text n. 2 while following along from text 1.

Exercise 1.3

Read the two texts, and complete the phrasal verbs and idiomatic expressions with their meaning.

Exercise 1.4

Listen to text n. 1 again, press pause after each sentence, and repeat.

Exercise 1.5

Put the correct preposition or particle next to the verb "BE", choosing among: OFF, UP, IN, AWAY, UP TO (x2), BACK, OVER.

BE OFF	BE UP TO (X2)	BE BACK	BE IN
BE UP	BE AWAY	BE OVER	

1) My husband _____ (is not here) at the moment. Could you call back, please?

2) I don't think this Monopoly game will _____ (end) soon. We'd better have some coffee.

3) I had a very salty pizza last night, and I _____ (was awake) the whole night drinking water.

4) A: What's the cat doing?

   B: I don't know, but he _____ (is about to do some mischief) no good!

5) Goodbye! I _____ (I'm leaving). I will _____ (be in another city) for the weekend. I will _____ (return) on Monday morning!

6) A: Should I get the black pants or the blue ones?

   B: I don't know... it _____ you (it's your decision). I think you look good in both.

Exercise 1.6

Put the correct preposition or particle next to the verb "BE", choosing among: *OFF, UP, IN, AWAY, UP TO (x2), BACK, OVER.*

1) Are the Spencers _____ ? I thought they were _____, but I can see that the lights are on at their house, so they must be _____ .

2) A: You look tired! What happened?

   B: Oh, I was _____ late last night because I had to finish my project, and didn't go to bed until it was _____.

3) A: Where's Jack?

   B: I don't know. He's _____ somewhere! He always disappears when it's time to do the dishes.

4) Our teenage daughter is _____ something! I can tell from the look on her face!

5) John looks very thoughtful. He's probably weighing the pros and cons about leaving his job for a new one, but we can't really advise him. It's entirely _____ him.

Exercise 1.7

Complete the dialogue with the following phrasal verbs: *Look for, Look after, Take (sb) on, Take on (sth).*

A: I'm sorry, I can't come to the party on Saturday. I have to 1) _____ (babysit) my little sister.

B: Wow, you're a real big sister. Being willing to 2) _____ (accept) such a responsibility!

A: Well, partly it's also because I need some petty cash. Rather than 3) _____ (searching for) and 4) _____ (hiring) a stranger, I figured I could do it.

B: Well, good for you.

Exercise 1.8

Complete the sentences with the following phrasal verbs: *Look for, Look after, Take (sb) on, Take on (sth).*

1) When I was working in England, my colleague asked me if I could _____ her cat while she was on vacation.

2) Have you heard? It seems that Sean was _____ by a famous tech company in Silicon Valley.

3) A: What are you _____?
   B: My glasses! Have you seen them?

4) When you graduate from school, will you just _____ any job, or will you try and be more selective?

Exercise 1.9

Complete the sentences using: Phrasal Verbs with BE + OFF, UP (x2), IN, AWAY, UP TO, BACK, OVER and Look for, Look after, Take (sb) on, Take on (sth).

1) Are you _____ Jason? He _____ (not). He will _____ shortly.

2) What _____ our toddler _____ with that crayon in his hand? He's standing too near the wall....

3) A: Could you _____ our plants while we _____ ? We will _____ tomorrow morning until Monday evening.

   B: Oh, I don't know if I should _____ that responsibility. You know I don't really have a green thumb.

   A: Oh, of course it _____ to you, but it would really be for just two days...

   B: Ok...

4) A. Why _____ you still _____ ? Isn't it a little late?

   B. I know, but I really need to finish this project by tomorrow, and I can't go to bed until it _____. If I do it well, they will _____ me _____, and I will have a new job!

Exercise 1.10

Look at Text 1 and write these sentences using an idiom, a phrase, or a collocation:

(BE) WELL OFF   BE IN SB'S SHOES

1) What would you do if you <u>were me</u> in this situation?

_____

2) James has recently bought a Rolls Royce. He must be fairly <u>wealthy</u>.

_____

CHAPTER 2: BREAK — EVERY CLOUD HAS A SILVER LINING

Text 1 🎧 3

One day, three years ago, Linda broke down at work when a colleague made her notice a mistake she had made.

The next day, she had to call in sick because she had broken out in a terrible rash. It wasn't surprising, considering how life hadn't exactly been all roses for her that year. First, someone had broken into her apartment while she was away, so she had to break her vacation off and go back home. Then she had broken up with her boyfriend, which really broke her heart back then. On top of that, her old car had broken down a couple of times, and she had to go to work on foot. After that incident at work, Linda had felt too embarrassed to go back to her office, and so she quit.

Nonetheless, every cloud has a silver lining. After giving up that job, she was taken on by a new company which offered her a better pay, and the cherry on top was that she met John, who is now her husband!

Text 2 🎧 4

One day, three years ago, Linda burst into tears at work when a colleague made her notice a mistake she had made.

The next day, she had to phone to say that she was sick because she had developed a sudden terrible rash. It wasn't surprising, considering how hard life had been on her that year. First, someone had entered her apartment while she was away, so she had to interrupt her vacation to return home. Then she had ended her relationship with her boyfriend, which made her feel really miserable back then. On top of that, her old car had stopped working a couple of times, and she had to go to work on foot. After that incident at work, Linda had felt too embarrassed to return to her office, and so she quit.

Nonetheless, every bad event carries something positive in it. After leaving that job, she was hired by a new company which offered her a better pay, and — best of all — she met John, who is now her husband!

Vocabulary

Break down (1) (phrasal verb) = _____

Call in (sick) (phrasal verb) = call a place (school, work) saying that you are sick

Break out (phrasal verb) = _____
[used for something unpleasant and potentially dangerous happening in a sudden, unexpected way: a war, a fight, a fire, an epidemic, a pandemic, a disease, a rash...]

Life isn't all roses (idiom) = _____

Break into (phrasal verb) = forcefully _____ somewhere

Break (sth) off (phrasal verb) = _____

Go back (phrasal verb)= _____

Break up (phrasal verb) = _____

Have your heart broken (idiom) = _____

Break sb's heart = make someone very sad

Break down (2) (phrasal verb) = _____

Every cloud has a silver lining (idiom) =

_____

Give up (phrasal verb) = _____
[1) stop doing something that you do regularly; 2) admitting defeat]

Take (sb) on (phrasal verb) = _____

The cherry on top (AmE) / The cherry on top of the cake (BrE) (idiom) =

_____

Exercise 2.1 🎧 3

Listen to text n. 1 while following along from text 2.

Exercise 2.2 🎧 4

Listen to text n. 2 while following along from text 1.

Exercise 2.3

Read the two texts, and complete the phrasal verbs and idiomatic expressions with their meaning.

Exercise 2.4

Listen to text n. 1 again, press pause after each sentence, and repeat.

Exercise 2.5

Put the correct preposition or particle next to the verb "BREAK", choosing among: DOWN (x2), UP, INTO, OFF, OUT.

BREAK DOWN (x2)	BREAK INTO	BREAK OUT
BREAK UP	BREAK OFF	

1) The fire _____ (suddenly started) in the middle of the night, but fortunately nobody got injured.

2) When the telephone rang, I had to _____ (interrupt) what I was doing and go answer.

3) Have you heard that Jason and Sarah have _____ (ended their relationship)? I would have never expected that.

4) When Thomas and Timothy were little, Timothy would _____ (enter though uninvited) Thomas's room and playfully distract him from studying.

5) Unfortunately, the taxi _____ (stopped working) in the middle of the highway, and the tourists missed their flight.

6) The elderly woman would easily _____ (start crying) when remembering about the good old days.

Exercise 2.6

Put the correct preposition or particle next to the verb "BREAK", choosing among: DOWN (x2), UP, INTO, OFF, OUT.

1) An epidemic broke _____ in China in December 2019. At the beginning, the rest of the world did not take it very seriously, but eventually every country had to break _____ their normal activities.

2) Has a bus ever broken _____ while you were on it?

3) Breaking _____ with your boyfriend or girlfriend is pretty common when you are a teenager. It breaks your heart, you break _____ , but then you grow stronger.

4) A: How dare you break _____ my room without knocking at the door and break my meditation _____?

   B: I'm sorry, everything was so quiet. I thought nobody was in.

Exercise 2.7

Complete the text with the following phrasal verbs:
Go back, Take (sb) on, Give up, Call in.

When I was a student I wanted to find a summer job in Ireland. I went to a touristy area in Dublin, and handed out my resumes to as many stores as I could. I was called by a gift shop with lots of tiny little knick knacks (decorative objects) with lots of different prices. I had to stand outside all day. The weather was extremely windy and unpredictable. After a week I got a flu, so I had to

1) _____ sick (phone to communicate something). The boss said that he liked me and he wanted to 2) _____ me _____ for the job (hire), but I didn't want to 3) _____ (return) and get sick again. Therefore, I thanked him, but 4) _____ it _____ (decline). I then found a job in a clothing store for that season.

Exercise 2.8

Complete the sentences with the following phrasal verbs: *Call in, Go back, Take (sb) on, Give up.*

1) Jack, Paul, and Mike had decided to go for a hike on the Appalachian trail and stay overnight. Unfortunately, Mike forgot to bring his sleeping bag, and they had to _____ in the afternoon.

2) Never _____ when you are learning something new! There are no mistakes: only feedback.

3) After a long search for the ideal candidate, the HR team was able to _____ the right person _____.

4) Pauline was stuck in traffic that day, so she had to _____ to work and warn that she would be late for the meeting.

Exercise 2.9

Complete the sentences using: Phrasal Verbs with BREAK +DOWN (x2), UP, INTO, OFF, OUT and Go back, Take (sb) on, Give up, Call in.

1) Last night I was reading a book while my mother was watching TV. Every five minutes she would comment on the film, _____ ing my reading _____ !

2) Jenny was so angry with Peter that she wanted to _____ with him, but he didn't _____ and convinced her to forgive him.

3) Yesterday, my computer _____ in the middle of working on my assignment, and I lost everything I had written!

4) She _____ in tears when she noticed that somebody had tried to _____ her apartment. She immediately _____ the crime to the police.

5) As the fight between the two cats _____, Nancy was quick enough to distract them with one of their toys.

6) I heard that they are _____ ing _____ new hairdressers at that hair salon. Why don't you send out your resume?

Exercise 2.10

Look at Text 1 and write these sentences using an idiom, a phrase, or a collocation:

LIFE ISN'T ALL ROSES   BREAK SB'S HEART

EVERY CLOUD HAS A SILVER LINING   THE CHERRY ON TOP

1) You made me really sad when you said that!

   _____

2) Cheer up! It's not as bad as it looks!

   _____

3) Life wasn't always so easy, but overall it wasn't too bad.

   _____

4) We had been enjoying our Christmas vacation meeting our friends and family. Then, even better, we found an offer to the Canary Islands, so we had an unexpected trip.

   _____

   _____

CHAPTER 3: CALL — GOOD GENES

Text 1 🎧 5

Jason lived about an hour away from his elderly mother, Margaret. Despite being almost ninety years old, she was as healthy as an ox: always active, cooking, cleaning, and gardening. Jason used to go and visit her at least once a week, or more if necessary.

Lately, though, Margaret had been acting up a little. For example, when Jason and his family had gone there for their usual lunch, the previous Sunday, she had looked impatient and rather happy when they had left.

During the week, he would call her up and find the answering machine on: he would leave a message, but she wouldn't call him back. He would then call up Dan, Margaret's neighbor, to ask if they had noticed anything unusual, but no, everything seemed fine to him. After a couple of days, he started to worry and he decided that the situation called for action! So, that evening he called off an appointment and just called in on her.

When he went in and saw that she wasn't around, he called her, but she wouldn't answer. He looked in the kitchen, in the dining room, in the living room. Everything was absolutely quiet. He was starting to worry. Then he heard her laughing. He found her in the knitting room, sitting by the window. That was puzzling: she was wearing a state-of-the-art set of wireless headphones connected to a tablet!

"Mom!", he shouted.

"Oh my goodness, dear! What are you doing here? Do you want to give me a heart-attack??"

Text 2 🎧 6

Jason lived about an hour away from his elderly mother, Margaret. Despite being almost ninety years old, she was very healthy: always active, cooking, cleaning, and gardening. Jason used to go and visit her at least once a week, or more if necessary.

Lately, though, Margaret had been behaving differently than usual. For example, when Jason and his family had gone there for their usual lunch, the previous Sunday, she had looked impatient and rather happy when they had left.

During the week, he would phone her and find the answering machine on: he would leave a message, but she wouldn't phone him in return. He would then phone Dan, Margaret's neighbor, to ask if they had noticed anything unusual, but no, everything seemed fine to him. After a couple of days, he started to worry and he decided that the situation required some action! So, that evening he cancelled an appointment and just visited her for a short time.

When he entered and saw that she wasn't around, he called her, but she wouldn't answer. He looked in the kitchen, in the dining room, in the living room. Everything was absolutely quiet. He was starting to worry. Then he heard her laughing. He found her in the knitting room, sitting by the window. That was puzzling: she was wearing an ultra-modern wireless set of headphones connected to a tablet!

"Mom!", he shouted.

"Oh my goodness, dear! What are you doing here? Do you want to give me a heart-attack??"

"What are you doing? Actually, what have you been

"What are you doing? Actually, what have you been doing? I've called you up many times but I couldn't get through to you... why didn't you call me back?"

"Oh dear! I think I'm in love!"

"What??"

"Dan, our neighbor... that adorable fellow... he said he's getting rid of superfluous things and gave me this amazing digital board..."

"It's a tablet."

"He taught me how to use it and if you press this button..."

"An icon."

"...you can access an entire digital library of audiobooks! It's like a miracle how so many books can fit in this little thing! I love spending my evenings listening to books! Right now I'm reading "Pride and Prejudice", by Jane Austen! It's marvelous! It's so engaging! I can't stop reading! And I'm already looking forward to reading the next one!" Her eyes were sparkling with joy and enthusiasm. Jason could't help but smiling in admiration and thinking: "Good genes... Thank you!

doing? I've phoned you many times but I couldn't contact you on the phone... why didn't you phone me in return?"

"Oh dear! I think I'm in love!"

"What??"

"Dan, our neighbor... that adorable fellow... he said he's eliminating superfluous things and gave me this amazing digital board..."

"It's a tablet."

"He taught me how to use it and if you press this button..."

"An icon."

"...you can access an entire digital library of audio-books! It's like a miracle how so many books can fit in this little thing! I love spending my evenings listening to books! Right now I'm reading "Pride and Prejudice", by Jane Austen! It's marvelous! It's so engaging! I can't stop reading! And I'm already feeling excited about reading the next one!"

Her eyes were sparkling with joy and enthusiasm. Jason couldn't help but smiling in admiration and thinking: "Good genes... Thank you!"

Vocabulary

Be as healthy as an ox (AmE) / horse (BrE) (idiom) =

_____

Act up (phrasal verb) = _____

Call (sb) up (phrasal verb) = _____

Call (sb) back (phrasal verb) = _____

Call for (sth) (phrasal verb) = _____

Call (sth) off (phrasal verb) = _____

Call in on (sb) (phrasal verb) = _____

Go in (phrasal verb) = _____

State-of-the-art (phrase) = _____

Get through to (sb) (phrasal verb) = _____

Get rid of (sth) (phrasal verb) = _____

Look forward to (sth) (phrasal verb) = _____

Exercise 3.1 🎧 5

Listen to text n. 1 while following along from text 2.

Exercise 3.2 🎧 6

Listen to text n. 2 while following along from text 1.

Exercise 3.3

Read the two texts, and complete the phrasal verbs and idiomatic expressions with their meaning.

Exercise 3.4

Listen to text n. 1 again, press pause after each sentence, and repeat.

Exercise 3.5

Put the correct preposition or particle next to the verb "CALL", choosing among: UP, OFF, FOR, IN ON, BACK.

CALL UP	CALL FOR	CALL BACK
CALL OFF	CALL IN ON	

1) I'm sorry, I have to _____ (cancel) our meeting due to an unforeseen commitment.

2) Hi, how are you? I was passing by, and I thought I could _____ (visit for a short time) you.

3) Mmmm... This soup _____ (needs) more salt.

4) They keep _____ ing him _____ (phone) but he never _____ them _____ (phones in return).

Exercise 3.6

Put the correct preposition or particle next to the verb "CALL", choosing among: UP, OFF, FOR, IN ON, BACK.

1) Your aunt is getting old. I think you should go and call _____ her more often.

2) The soccer match was called _____ due to bad weather.

3) That's great news! Congratulations! This calls _____ champagne!

4) I got an email from Sonia. I guess I'll just call her _____ , so it's quicker.

5) I found a phone call from my dad. I'm going to call him _____.

Exercise 3.7

Complete the text with the following phrasal verbs: *Act up, Go in, Get through to (sb), Get rid of, Look forward to.*

It was time to 1) _____ (eliminate) my old smartphone. It had been 2) _____ ing _____ (doing strange things) recently. As a result, I couldn't 3) _____ (contact on the phone) anybody. So, that Saturday I went to the electronic appliances store. I 4) _____ (entered), and I bought a real state-of-the-art smartphone. I'm really excited! I'm 5) _____ trying it out!

Exercise 3.8

Complete the sentences with the following phrasal verbs: *Act up, Go in, Get through to (sb), Get rid of, Look forward to.*

1) A: Why don't we _____ this old bicycle? It's hopelessly broken.

   B: Do you think so? I think we can still have it fixed...

2) You've been _____ recently... is there anything wrong? Perhaps I can help you, even just by listening...

CHAPTER 3: CALL — GOOD GENES

3) I don't want to _____ there. You go. I'll wait here.

4) Jeff is _____ his Christmas vacation. This year he's going to spend it in the Philippines.

5) Did you _____ Mr. Thomson and forward my message?

Exercise 3.9

Complete the sentences using: Phrasal Verbs with CALL + OFF, UP, BACK, IN ON, FOR and *Go in, Act up, Get through to (sb), Get rid of.*

1) Last week I had scheduled a meeting with my friend, but I had to _____ it _____ because I got sick.

2) The computer has been _____ ing _____ . I'm afraid it might have a bug.

3) The pandemic _____ everybody's sense of discipline and responsibility in trying to contain its spread as much as possible.

4) Jessica has been looking at clothes in that store for ages. Mark has been waiting outside. He's been trying to _____ her _____ to tell her to hurry, but since he can't _____ her, I think he'll soon _____ and tell her in person.

5) Paul hadn't seen his grandma in a long time, and since he was passing by her house, he decided to _____ her. She was really happy to see him.

6) (On the phone) A: "Hello?"
   B: "Hello, could you _____ me _____ in about ten minutes, please? I'm driving at the moment.."
   A: "Ok, no problem. Drive safely."

7) A: "Hey, do you need a desk? We're _____ it if nobody wants it. It's still in good condition, but we need to buy a bigger one now that our daughter is growing."
   B: "Well, I'll have a look at it. Thank you."

Exercise 3.10

Look at Text 1 and write these sentences using an idiom, a phrase, or a collocation:

STATE-OF-THE-ART   AS HEALTHY AS AN OX

1) Your child really looks nice and healthy. That's good!

   _____

2) The ultra-modern "HMS Warrior", built in 1860, was the first ironclad warship: a huge technological advance that made it unbeatable.

   _____

CHAPTER 4: CARRY — A SPECIAL FRIENDSHIP

Text 1 🎧 7

Mark came back home from school, and as always, before sitting at the table, he made sure to look around and listen carefully, but no, nothing today either!

He went to the kitchen and crossed out another day on the calendar: so far in total Philip had been missing for twenty days.

Philip was his best friend: an adorable, cheerful, black and white border collie. Everybody loved him in town. He was excellent at carrying out his routines at the dog training school; he could carry off even the most difficult tasks! Mark and his family were proud of him!

One of the tasks Philip had been trained to do before going missing was carrying the newspaper around the neighborhood from the newsstand all the way home. People loved seeing him doing that.

He had become so good at it, that Mark's father had started to trust him enough to send him on his own.

Philip, though, was still relatively young, and probably had been distracted by something, the day he disappeared. That day, in fact, he never made it to the newsstand. Anything could have happened: he may have been taken away, or hit by a car. The thought of him being injured or even passed away gave the whole family the shivers.

It was as if he had vanished into thin air. Mark was heartbroken. He would often be carried back by sweet memories of his best friend, and found it difficult to get down to doing his homework.

Mark's parents had put up missing notices

Text 2 🎧 8

Mark returned home from school, and as always, before sitting at the table, he made sure to look around and listen carefully, but no, nothing today either!

He went to the kitchen and erased another day from the calendar: so far in total Philip had been missing for twenty days.

Philip was his best friend: an adorable, cheerful, black and white border collie. Everybody loved him in town. He was excellent at performing his routines at the dog training school; he could execute successfully even the most difficult tasks! Mark and his family were proud of him!

One of the tasks Philip had been trained to do before going missing was holding the newspaper in his mouth and taking it around the neighborhood from the newsstand all the way home. People loved seeing him doing that. He had become so good at it, that Mark's father had started to trust him enough to send him on his own.

Philip, though, was still relatively young, and probably had been distracted by something, the day he disappeared. That day, in fact, he never made it to the newsstand. Anything could have happened: he may have been taken by somebody, or hit by a car. The thought of him being injured or even dead made the whole family feel very bad.

It was as if he had totally disappeared. Mark was heartbroken. He would often be brought back in time by sweet memories of his best friend, and found it difficult to concentrate on his homework.

Mark's parents had put up missing notices

everywhere, but so far nobody had claimed him. They were starting to lose hope, but most of all they were concerned about Mark, and were trying to help him to <u>get over this</u> and <u>carry on with</u> his life.

One Saturday morning, while Mark was still in school, a truck driver rang at the door bell. He had brought a dog with him. He didn't even need to say anything because the dog immediately jumped out of his arms, and everybody's joy was uncontainable! Philip was back!

"I found this adorable fellow at the highway entrance ramp about 25 days ago. I was afraid he might get injured and I took him with me, but it was clear since the beginning that he belonged to someone. I didn't manage to come back around to this area sooner, but today the moment I saw the missing notices, I <u>called in on you</u> right away! He's been a very good travel fellow for me, but he's obviously happier here where he belongs!"

Mark's parents were immensely grateful and they offered him a reward, but he refused. Later on, when Mark came home, he found the sweetest surprise ever! When the two best friends met again, <u>they were over the moon</u> with joy, and the house was a place of playfulness and laughter again!

everywhere, but so far nobody had claimed him. They were starting to lose hope, but most of all they were concerned about Mark, and were trying to help him to <u>recover from this</u> and <u>continue</u> living his life.

One Saturday morning, while Mark was still in school, a truck driver rang at the door bell. He had brought a dog with him. He didn't even need to say anything because the dog immediately jumped out of his arms, and everybody's joy was uncontainable! Philip was back!

"I found this adorable fellow at the highway entrance ramp about 25 days ago. I was afraid he might get injured and I took him with me, but it was clear since the beginning that he belonged to someone. I didn't manage to come back around to this area sooner, but today the moment I saw the missing notices, I <u>came to visit you</u> right away! He's been a very good travel fellow for me, but he's obviously happier here where he belongs!"

Mark's parents were immensely grateful and they offered him a reward, but he refused. Later on, when Mark came home, he found the sweetest surprise ever! When the two best friends met again, <u>they were overwhelmed with joy</u>, and the house was a place of playfulness and laughter again!

Vocabulary

Come back (phrasal verb) = _____

Cross (sth) out (phrasal verb) = _____

Carry (sth) out (phrasal verb) = _____

Carry (sth) off (phrasal verb) = _____

Carry (sth) around (phrasal verb) = _____

Take away (phrasal verb) = move someone/something from one place to another

Pass away (phrasal verb) = _____

Give (sb) the shivers (idiom) = _____

Vanish into thin air (idiom) = _____

Carry (sb) back (to sth) (phrasal verb) =

_____

Get down to (sth) (phrasal verb) = _____

Get over (sth) (phrasal verb) = _____

Carry on (with sth) (phrasal verb) = _____

Call in on (phrasal verb) = _____

Be over the moon (idiom) = _____

Exercise 4.1 🎧 7

Listen to text n. 1 while following along from text 2.

Exercise 4.2 🎧 8

Listen to text n. 2 while following along from text 1.

Exercise 4.3

Read the two texts, and complete the phrasal verbs and idiomatic expressions with their meaning.

Exercise 4.4

Listen to text n. 1 again, press pause after each sentence, and repeat.

Exercise 4.5

Put the correct preposition or particle next to the verb "CARRY", choosing among: OUT, OFF, AROUND, ON, BACK.

CARRY OUT   CARRY AROUND   CARRY BACK
CARRY OFF   CARRY ON

1) When she heard that song, she was suddenly _____ (brought back) to high school memories.

2) There's a difference between _____ ing _____ (executing) and passing an overall easy test, and _____ ing _____ (executing successfully) a super difficult test.

3) Sorry, I broke you off while you were speaking. Please, _____ (continue).

4) Why are you always _____ ing _____ two bags with you? Isn't one bag enough?

Exercise 4.6

Put the correct preposition or particle next to the verb "CARRY", choosing among: OUT, OFF, AROUND, ON, BACK.

1) What were you saying? I was carried _____ by the smell of lasagna. It reminds me of when I was a child.

2) It's important to carry _____ stirring the béchamel sauce, or else it sticks to the pot.

3) That was her first presentation in public. She was very nervous, but she carried it _____ in an excellent way. Everybody was enthusiastic .

4) Linus always carries _____ his beloved blanket. (From the comic strip books *Peanuts* by Charles M. Schulz)

5) After carrying _____ market research, we felt more confident in placing the product in this area.

Exercise 4.7

Complete the sentences with the following phrasal verbs: *Come back, Take away, Cross out, Pass away, Call in on, Get down to, Get over.*

1) "Bye, I'm off. I don't know what time I'll _____ ." (return).

2) The tenant who lived here before us was an elderly man who _____ (died) two years ago after moving to a retirement home.

3) A: "What? That's my sweater! You can't _____ (take) things _____ from people without asking!"
B: "Oh, but it's so nice! It looks great on me!"

4) Ok, let's have a quick lunch, and then let's _____ (concentrate on) business.

5) While grocery shopping: "Ok, mayonnaise, here we go. You can _____ that _____ (erase) from the list, thank you."

6) After the earthquake in Northern Italy in 1976, many people found it very difficult to _____ (recover from) the shock.

7) A: "Have you heard from Lucy and Harry?"

B: "No, in fact I'd like to _____ (go for a visit) them after work. Would you like to come along?"

Exercise 4.8

Complete the sentences with the following phrasal verbs: *Come back, Take away, Cross out, Pass away, Call in on, Get down to, Get over*.

1) Read the words and _____ the odd one.

2) What are you waiting for? _____ work! You need to study hard if you want to pass your test tomorrow!

3) Don't leave the plastic bag near the stove! _____ it _____ from there! It can catch fire!

4) "Please, _____ ! I can't live without you!", said Mr Kovalyov to his nose. (From the short story *The Nose* by Nikolai Gogol)

5) It was a very bad flu, but fortunately he's _____ ing _____ it.

6) As soon as they learned that Mr. Moore had _____, they immediately went to express their condolences to his family members.

7) Steve liked Anne. Whenever he had the chance, he would _____ her with an excuse. She didn't mind his visits.

Exercise 4.9

Complete the sentences using: Phrasal Verbs with CARRY + OUT, OFF, AROUND, BACK, ON and Come back, Cross out, Take away, Call in on, Pass away, Get down to, Get over.

1) After he _____, it was very difficult for everyone to _____ it and _____ with life.

2) Toddlers can be incredibly fast. They need to be looked after carefully and _____ from potentially dangerous places.

3) Read the multiple choices in the exercise and _____ the incorrect option.

4) "Come on, you two! Stop chatting and _____ some studying."

5) I was a bit confused when my daughter today _____ home, _____ing _____ a teddy bear... I asked her about it, but she smiled and said nothing... Could she be in love?

6) They _____ the experiment in total secret.

7) Jack had a very challenging job interview yesterday, but he _____ it _____ very successfully. In fact he was taken on.

8) A: "Hi, how is it going? I decided to _____ you to see how you were..."
   B: "It was a very good idea. Come in!"

Exercise 4.10

Look at Text 1 and write these sentences using an idiom, a phrase, or a collocation:

BE OVER THE MOON   GIVE SB THE SHIVERS   VANISH INTO THIN AIR

1) Where are my glasses? I've been looking for them the whole morning. It's as if they had disappeared. I hope I didn't lose them.

   _____

   _____

2) Henry and Sally were overjoyed when their baby was born.

   _____

3) I'm really afraid of spiders; just the thought of seeing one makes me feel terrified.

   _____

CHAPTER 5: COME — AT THE STROKE OF MIDNIGHT

Text 1 🎧 9

Helen was heartbroken when she found that the dress she had come into upon her mother's death had now come apart. She couldn't understand how this could have come about! Now it was absolutely impossible for her to go to The Grand Ball! She was so desperate that she broke down in tears! Suddenly, out of the blue, the Fairy Godmother appeared. She tried to cheer her up, but poor Helen was really down in the dumps. So, the Fairy Godmother came up with an idea that would have surely made Helen come round to a different attitude!

With the wave of her magic wand, she turned a pumpkin she had come across into a wonderful limousine, a mouse into a chauffeur, and her pajamas into the most beautiful designer dress with crystal stiletto shoes! Now she was ready to go to The Grand Ball! "But," the Fairy Godmother warned, "The spell will break at the stroke of midnight."

RING RING RING! Helen woke up!

"Was it midnight?" she thought.

"Helen! It's time to get up! Good morning! You were really sound asleep!" said Helen's mother.

"Oh mom! I'm so happy you're alive!" Helen thought while looking around still half asleep in her pajamas. "Oh, it was just a dream…. But it felt so real…."

She got up. What was a pumpkin doing on her desk..?

Text 2 🎧 10

Helen was heartbroken when she found that the dress she had inherited upon her mother's death had now broken into pieces. She couldn't understand how this could have occurred! Now it was absolutely impossible for her to go to The Grand Ball! She was so desperate that she burst into tears! Suddenly, out of nowhere, the Fairy Godmother appeared. She tried to uplift her, but poor Helen was really depressed. So, the Fairy Godmother had an idea that would have surely made Helen change her mind and acquire a different attitude!

With the help of her magic wand, she transformed a pumpkin she had found by chance into a wonderful limousine, a mouse into a chauffeur, and her pajamas into the most beautiful designer dress with crystal stiletto shoes! Now she was ready to go to The Grand Ball! "But," the Fairy Godmother warned, "The spell will cease its effect exactly at midnight."

RING RING RING! Helen awoke!

"Was it midnight?" she thought.

"Helen! It's time to get out of bed! Good morning! You were really in a deep sleep!" said Helen's mother.

"Oh mom! I'm so happy you're alive!" Helen thought while looking around still half asleep in her pajamas. "Oh, it was just a dream…. But it felt so real…."

She got up. What was a pumpkin doing on her desk..?

Vocabulary:

Come into (sth) (phrasal verb) = _____

Come apart (phrasal verb) = _____

Come about (phrasal verb) = _____

Break down (phrasal verb) = _____

Out of the blue (idiom)= _____

Cheer (sb) up (phrasal verb) = _____

Be down in the dumps (idiom) = _____

Come up with (an idea) (phrasal verb) =

_____

Come round to (sth) (phrasal verb) = _____

With the wave of the magic wand (idiom) =

_____

Turn (sth/sb) into (phrasal verb) = _____

Come across (sth/sb) (phrasal verb) =

_____

Break the spell (idiom) = _____

At the stroke of (idiom) = _____

Wake (sb) up (phrasal verb) = _____

Get up (phrasal verb) = _____

Be sound asleep (phrase) = _____

Come round/ come over (phrasal verb) =

_____

Exercise 5.1 🎧 9

Listen to text n. 1 while following along from text 2.

Exercise 5.2 🎧 10

Listen to text n. 2 while following along from text 1.

Exercise 5.3

Read the two texts, and complete the phrasal verbs and idiomatic expressions with their meaning.

Exercise 5.4

Listen to text n. 1 again, press pause after each sentence, and repeat.

Exercise 5.5

Put the correct preposition or particle next to the verb "COME", choosing among: INTO, APART, ABOUT, UP WITH, ROUND TO, ROUND/OVER, ACROSS.

COME INTO	COME ABOUT	COME ROUND TO	COME ACROSS
COME APART	COME UP WITH	COME ROUND/OVER	

1) The speed at which technological advances have _____ (happened/ occurred) in the last two decades is just incredible!

2) Peter was having a walk in a field nearby when he _____ (found by change) a sleeping raccoon all curled up like a cat.

3) Do you still think that our math teacher is cool, or have you _____ (changed idea) a different opinion after today's boring lesson?

4) Mmmm… this is a problem! We have to _____ (have/ find) a solution as soon as possible!

5) My host mother had cooked the spaghetti for so long that when she drained it, it was _____ ing _____ (breaking/ falling into pieces).

6) Why don't you _____ (visit us) one of these days? We'll show you our new apartment!

7) Samuel _____ (inherited) a very big amount of money from a distant relative he had never met.

Exercise 5.6

Put the correct preposition or particle next to the verb "COME", choosing among: APART, ABOUT, ROUND TO, OVER/ROUND, UP WITH, INTO, ACROSS.

1) I came _____ Lauren the other day. She says hello.

2) This old leather jacket is coming _____ ! I can't wear it any more...

3) At first, Jackie didn't want to move house, but after discussing it with Andrew, she came _____ a different perspective.

4) Our friends come _____ every Saturday night, and we play a board game! Susan came _____ this idea once, and we had so much fun that we made it into a tradition!

5) Robert and his relatives came _____ some money and a house when their uncle passed away.

6) I don't know how it came _____... we were just best friends and then we fell in love.

Exercise 5.7

Complete the sentences with the following phrasal verbs:

Break down (2), Cheer up, Turn into, Wake up, Get up, Come round/over.

1) Could you please _____ me _____ (awake) tomorrow morning? Or else, I'll never _____ (get out of bed).

2) Unfortunately, the washing machine _____ (stopped working) at a time when we didn't have enough money to replace it.

3) When her father left by train, the little girl _____ (started to cry) in tears. Her mother had to buy her an ice-cream to _____ her _____ (uplift).

4) With lots of work and dedication, Jack _____ the shack _____ (transform) a very cosy house shed.

5) When are you _____ ing _____ (visiting)? Your father and I miss you, now that you are at college.

Exercise 5.8

Complete the text with the following phrasal verbs:

Break down, Cheer up, Turn into, Wake up, Get up, Come over, Come round.

That day, Sophie 1) _____ and immediately 2) _____ full of energy. She was in a very good mood because her grandparents were 3) _____ ing _____ after a really long time. She had 4) _____ a beautiful young lady: she was tall and slender now... She still remembered the last time grandma had 5) _____ : she was still short and a little chubby. When she had come home from school, she had 6) _____ in tears because of a stupid classmate. Grandma had hugged her and sweetly 7) _____ her _____. Now that class-mate was rather interested in Sophie, but she didn't even look at him!

Exercise 5.9

Complete the sentences using: Phrasal Verbs with COME + APART, ABOUT, ROUND TO, OVER/ROUND, UP WITH, INTO, ACROSS, and *Break down, Cheer up, Turn into, Wake up, Get up.*

1) The book from the school library had totally _____ after the dog had bitten into it. I apologized to the school library, and bought a new one.

2) Sarah initially didn't like her colleagues, but after knowing them better, she _____ a different opinion of them.

3) (On the phone) Merry Christmas to you all! Everybody _____ for dinner here. We're having fun! What about you?

4) Sometimes, it's good to give yourself a little treat to _____ you _____ after a bad day.

5) I was looking for our usual hotel when I _____ this new one, which looks really great and has very good prices.

6) When Marie was younger, she would easily _____ over little things. She was a little spoiled.

7) John was sleeping really nicely when the dog bark _____ him _____.

8) Old Uncle Tim's death _____ a big surprise for his nephews and nieces: they _____ quite a large amount of money, which they hadn't expected. So they felt very thankful to him.

9) You _____ nice and early this morning! That's unusual! How did this _____?

Exercise 5.10

Look at Text 1 and write these sentences using an idiom, a phrase, or a collocation:

BREAK THE SPELL   BE DOWN IN THE DUMPS

AT THE STROKE OF   BE SOUND ASLEEP

WITH THE WAVE OF   OUT OF THE BLUE

1) He was a very authoritative teacher. He was able to bring peace and quiet in class just by lifting his finger!

_____

_____

2) We were enjoying the romantic landscape, but then a car beeping ruined the moment.

_____

_____

3) Don't talk to him today! He's depressed because his favorite team lost, yesterday.

_____

_____

4) Billy was a very faithful and punctual dog! Every day at exactly 5:00 pm, it would be outside of Jack's office, waiting for him.

_____

_____

5) She was deeply asleep on the sofa when, suddenly, her brother shouted, "Goal!"

_____

_____

CHAPTER 6: FALL — KEEP YOUR SPIRITS HIGH!

Text 1 🎧 11

That was it! That was truly <u>the straw that broke the camel's back!</u> Mandy couldn't take it any more. Everything was <u>falling apart</u> in that office! She had been <u>taken on</u> six months before as a manager to organize things better, and find a solution to the company's problems. Her boss had promised his complete support for any <u>idea she would come up with</u>. Mandy had done her best, but after <u>falling out</u> once again with her boss over the fact that he adamantly refused to upgrade the computers, she finally realized how she had <u>fallen for his promises</u>. How could she improve the situation if he never <u>gave her the green light to</u> her proposals? It was no wonder that his employees constantly <u>fell behind schedule</u>. This, in turn, <u>brought about</u> constant dissatisfaction among the customers. <u>Talking to her boss was like talking to a brick wall</u>: he just wouldn't listen. The situation was <u>utterly</u> <u>frustrating</u>, and she was on the verge of <u>falling apart</u>.

That day, she realized that it just <u>wasn't worth it</u>, and she quit her job.

She could always <u>fall back on</u> her customer care skills and find a temporary position in a store. This job had been a rather low point in her career. Her attempts in <u>carrying out her tasks</u> had <u>fallen through</u> quite miserably.

But never mind.

She just had to <u>keep her spirits high</u> and <u>play it by ear</u> for a while. Sooner or later, she would <u>figure things out</u> and find her path in life again.

Text 2 🎧 12

That was it! That was truly <u>the last of a series of outrageous episodes that had been happening!</u> Mandy could not bear it any more. Everything was <u>broken or disintegrating</u> in that office! She had been <u>hired</u> six months prior as a manager to organize things better, and find a solution to the company's problems. Her boss had promised his complete support for any <u>idea she would have</u>. Mandy had done her best, but after <u>quarreling</u> once again with her boss over the fact that he adamantly refused to upgrade the computers, she finally realized how she had <u>believed his false</u> <u>promises</u>. How could she improve the situation if he <u>never agreed on</u> anything she proposed? It was no wonder that his employees could never <u>meet the deadlines</u>. This, in turn, <u>caused</u> constant dissatisfaction amongst the customers. <u>Talking to</u> her boss was impossible: he just would not listen. This situation was <u>terribly</u> frustrating, and she was on the verge of a <u>nervous breakdown</u>.

That day, she realized that it just <u>was not worth the effort</u>, and she resigned from her job.

She could always <u>have recourse to</u> her customer care skills and find a temporary position in a store. This job had been a rather low point in her career. Her attempts in <u>completing her tasks</u> had <u>failed</u> quite miserably.

But never mind.

She just had to <u>remain optimistic</u> and <u>deal with the situation day by day</u> for a while. Sooner or later, she would <u>understand</u> what her path in life was.

Vocabulary:

The straw that broke the camel's back (idiom) =

_____

Fall apart (1) (phrasal verb) = _____

Take (sb) on (phrasal verb) = _____

Come up with (an idea) (phrasal verb) =

_____

Fall out (with sb) (phrasal verb) = _____

Fall for (phrasal verb) = _____

Give the green light (idiom) = _____

Fall behind (schedule) (phrasal verb) =

_____

Bring about (phrasal verb) = _____

It's like talking to a brick wall (idiom) =

_____

Utterly frustrating (collocation) = _____

Fall apart (2) (phrasal verb) = _____

(Not) be worth it (idiom) = _____

Fall back on (sth) = _____

Carry out (phrasal verb) = _____

Fall through (phrasal verb) = _____

Keep one's spirits high/up (idiom) = _____

Play it by ear (idiom) = _____

Figure (sth) out (phrasal verb) = _____

Exercise 6.1 🎧 11

Listen to text n. 1 while following along from text 2.

Exercise 6.2 🎧 12

Listen to text n. 2 while following along from text 1.

Exercise 6.3

Read the two texts, and complete the phrasal verbs and idiomatic expressions with their meaning.

Exercise 6.4

Listen to text n. 1 again, press pause after each sentence, and repeat.

Exercise 6.5

Put the correct preposition or particle next to the verb "FALL", choosing among: APART (x2), OUT, FOR, BEHIND, IN, BACK ON, THROUGH.

FALL APART (x2)	FALL FOR	FALL BACK ON
FALL OUT	FALL BEHIND	FALL THROUGH

1) Are you sure it's safe to use your car? It's practically _____ ing _____ (disintegrating). No offense meant.

2) Since all his plans for the vacation _____ (failed) due to the bad weather, he had to come up with other ideas.

3) A naive person is a person who tends to _____ (believe) everything people tell them.

4) I hate _____ ing _____ schedule (not meeting deadlines).

5) After the two friends _____ (quarreled), they stopped talking for years. Fortunately, now they have made up with each other.

6) If worst come to worst, I can always _____ (have recourse) my artistic skills and sell my art.

7) After the divorce, he really _____ (had a nervous breakdown).

Exercise 6.6

Put the correct preposition or particle next to the verb "FALL", choosing among: APART (x2), OUT, FOR, BEHIND, BACK ON, THROUGH (x2).

1) The cat tried to catch the bird, but its attempts fell _____ miserably.

2) Unfortunately, some people are prone to fall _____ scams.

3) Falling _____ with someone is always a pretty serious matter that most of the time can be avoided.

4) Mary has fallen _____ schedule with the ironing, and now she has to ask for her mother's help.

5) My son thinks that if he falls _____ at school, he can always fall _____ his basketball skills and become some sort of champion.

6) If it hadn't been for yoga and meditation, he would have fallen _____ a long time ago. His job is very stressful.

Exercise 6.7

Complete the sentences with the following phrasal verbs:

Take (sb) on, Come up with, Bring about, Carry out, Figure (sth) out.

1) Covid 19 has _____ (caused) a big change in the work market. A lot more people work from home now.

2) We need to _____ (find, create) a solution, and _____ this _____ (understand).

3) My father is looking for somebody to _____ (hire) as an engineer in his company.

4) Your daughter is very diligent. She always _____ (complete, execute) her assignments precisely and in a timely manner.

Exercise 6.8

Complete the text with the following phrasal verbs:

Take (sb) on, Come up with, Bring about, Carry out, Figure (sth) out.

In some countries, Covid 19 1) _____ lots of unemployment, but due to government stimulus checks, it became paradoxically difficult to 2) _____ somebody _____. It was somehow more profitable for people to stay at home than 3) _____ ing _____ their duties at work for very little money. Companies had a hard time in 4) _____ ing things _____. They probably 5) _____ all sorts of perks to attract workforce back.

CHAPTER 6: FALL — KEEP YOUR SPIRITS HIGH!

Exercise 6.9

Complete the sentences using: Phrasal Verbs with FALL + APART (x2), OUT, FOR, BEHIND, BACK ON, THROUGH, and *Take (sb) on, Come up with, Bring about, Carry out (x2), Figure (sth) out (x2).*

1) That book is literally _____ ing _____ ! You have to _____ something _____ to fix it.

2) Lauren is such a creative person! She's always _____ ing _____ creative ideas to make her business thrive. Her creativity is a skill she can always _____ in case things go badly.

3) That episode _____ a profound shift in perspective for many people.

4) The problem of not _____ ing _____ your tasks timely is that then you _____ schedule, and this can be stressful.

5) Your secretary _____ too many duties for one person. If you don't _____ some-body _____, she will _____.

6) My son is going to take a month off from work, and he is going to travel around Europe. He is hop-ing that this journey will help him to _____ things _____ with his life.

7) When the two brothers _____ with each other, their mother's attempts to bring them together again _____ miserably, at first.

Exercise 6.10

Look at Text 1 and write these sentences using an idiom, a phrase, or a collocation:

THE LAST STRAW THAT BROKE THE CAMEL'S BACK	IT'S LIKE (TALKING TO) A BRICK WALL
UTTERLY FRUSTRATING	PLAY IT BY EAR
(NOT) BE WORTH IT	KEEP YOUR SPIRITS HIGH
	GIVE THE GREEN LIGHT

1) We never plan anything ahead for our vacation. We like to decide minute by minute.

_____

_____

2) That was the last of a long series of outrageous behavior. I'm extremely angry and I'm leaving!

_____

_____

3) It's when things go badly that you need to remain optimistic the most.

_____

_____

4) I know it's terribly frustrating talking to someone who doesn't listen.

_____

_____

5) We tried really hard, but honestly it wasn't worth the effort.

_____

_____

6) Mark asked his aunt if we can have the party in her beach apartment, and she said yes to him.

_____

_____

CHAPTER 7: DROP/GET— A TEMPEST IN A TEAPOT

Text 1 🎧 13

Grandma was very worried about Peter. He was a bright young thing. He had always been a cheerful boy, always getting along well with everybody. In the last few days, however, he had looked quite heavy-hearted. Something was troubling him. So, today when Peter dropped in for a visit, grandma delicately asked, "What's on your mind, Peter? I can tell that a storm is brewing, there."

Peter smiled bitterly, "Grandma, the world isn't what I thought it was. Grandma, I think I'm going to drop out of school."

Grandma couldn't believe her own ears! "Dropping out of school? You're a senior this year. In a couple of months you'll be out anyways! You've always been an excellent student! What's this all about?"

"Grandma, I need to. My best friend Mike has been going through trouble with this kid in school... he's always so bossy and overbearing.

"One day, we were playing a soccer match. He came down on Mike like a brick wall just because he made the team lose. Mike can't get over the humiliation and has called in sick since that day. I know that he's considering never going back to school again and even dropping out. My friends and I tried to talk Mike out of his decision, but we can't get this across to him. And as for this kid, how could he storm at Mike like that and get away with it? No, grandma. If Mike drops out, I'm going to drop out too! That's final!"

"Grandma listened carefully. Then she said, "Peter, dear. I understand that the whole situation makes your blood boil. However, I don't entirely see eye

Text 2 🎧 14

Grandma was very concerned about Peter. He was so young and enthusiastic. He had always been a cheerful boy, and had always been friends with everybody. However, in the last few days he had looked quite sad and thoughtful. Something was troubling him. So, today when Peter went for a visit, grandma delicately inquired, "What have you been thinking about, Peter? I can tell that something has been troubling you."

Peter smiled bitterly, "Grandma, the world isn't what I thought it was. Grandma, I think I'm going to leave school."

Grandma was extremely surprised! "Leaving school? You're at your final year. You'll have finished soon in any case! You've always been such an excellent student! Why are thinking about this, now?"

"Grandma, I must. My best friend Mike has been having problems with a classmate in school... he's always so despotic and domineering.

"One day, we were playing a soccer match. He rebuked Mike very harshly just because he made the team lose. Mike isn't able to overcome the humiliation and since that day he hasn't come to school saying that he's sick. I know that he's considering never going back to school again and even leaving. My friends and I tried to convince Mike that this was a bad decision, but we can't make him understand our point. And as for this classmate of ours, how could he address Mike so angrily and aggressively and go unpunished? No, grandma. If Mike leaves the school, I'm going to quit too! That's my final decision!"

to eye with Mike's decision. You can't get away from hurdles. Life will always be full of them. The students' families need to join forces and discretely get through to the school principal and make him aware of the situation.

"As far as this arrogant kid... you can't just get rid of him with a punishment. This will only hurt his feelings and pride, and I don't think he'll learn his lesson. No, he needs to be loved, included in some constructive project, possibly in a field where Mike shines and can even help him out. What do you think? If you want we can go and talk to mom and dad about this."

"Ok grandma, I'm in!", said Peter.

"But then promise me that you'll get down to studying seriously again! It's your last year. It would be nice if you could not only get through, but pass with flying colors! If all goes well, one day, you will all remember this incident as a tempest in a teapot!"

Grandma listened carefully. Then she said, "Peter, dear. I understand that the whole situation makes you really furious. However, I don't entirely agree with Mike's decision. You can't avoid obstacles. Life will always be full of them. The students' families need to gather together and discretely contact the school principal and make him aware of the situation.

"As far as this arrogant student... you can't just dispose of him with a punishment. This will only hurt his feelings and pride, and I don't think he'll learn his lesson. No, he needs to be loved, included in some constructive project, possibly in a field where Mike is very good and can even help him. What do you think? If you want we can go and talk to mom and dad about this."

"Ok, Grandma, I like this plan! Let's do it!", said Peter.

"But then promise me that you'll start to study seriously again! It's your last year. It would be nice if you could not only just pass, but pass with honors (successfully)! If all goes well, one day, you will all remember this incident as a big deal over nothing!

Vocabulary

A bright young thing (idiom) = _____

Get on/along with (sb) (phrasal verb) =

_____

Heavy-hearted (collocation) = _____

Drop in (phrasal verb) = _____

A storm is brewing (idiom) = _____
[trouble or a negative situation is about to happen or developing with potential negative consequences]

Drop out (of school) (phrasal verb) = _____

Not believe one's (own) ears (idiom) =

_____

Go through (trouble) (phrasal verb) = _____

Come down on (sb) (phrasal verb) = _____

Get over (sth) (phrasal verb) = _____

Call in (sick) (phrasal verb) = _____

Talk (sb) out (of sth) (phrasal verb) = _____

Get (sth) across (to sb) (phrasal verb) =

_____

Storm (at sb) (idiom) = _____

Get away with (sth) (phrasal verb) = _____

That's final! (phrase) = _____

Sth makes one's blood boil (idiom) = _____

See eye to eye with sb (idiom) = _____

Get away from (sth) (phrasal verb) = _____

Join forces (collocation) = _____
[to achieve a common goal]

Get through to (sb) (phrasal verb) = _____

Get rid of (sth/sb) (phrasal verb) = _____

Help (sb) out (phrasal verb) = _____

Be in (phrase) = _____

Get down to (work, studying, etc.) (phrasal verb) =

_____

Get through (phrasal verb) = _____

Pass with flying colors (idiom) = _____

A tempest in a teapot (AmE) / A storm in a teacup (BrE) (idiom) =

_____

Exercise 7.1 🎧 13

Listen to text n. 1 while following along from text 2.

Exercise 7.2 🎧 14

Listen to text n. 2 while following along from text 1.

Exercise 7.3

Read the two texts, and complete the phrasal verbs and idiomatic expressions with their meaning.

Exercise 7.4

Listen to text n. 1 again, press pause after each sentence, and repeat.

Exercise 7.5

Put the correct preposition or particle next to the verb "GET", choosing among: RID OF, ON/ALONG, OVER, AWAY WITH, AWAY FROM, DOWN TO, THROUGH, THROUGH TO, ACROSS TO.

GET RID OF	GET AWAY WITH	GET THROUGH
GET ON/ALONG	GET AWAY FROM	GET THROUGH TO
GET OVER	GET DOWN TO	GET ACROSS TO

1) Unfortunately, Lauren can't seem to _____ (overcome) her breakup with Paul. Let's invite her to go out with us more often.

2) A: Are you still using this notebook?
   B: No, you can _____ it (throw it, dispose of it).

3) I _____ (be friends with) well with my sister and my parents. We are a close-knit family.

4) It's incredible how Neil always _____ (pass) his tests without ever even studying. He always _____ it (go unpunished).

5) Ok, I loved our tea together, but now we need to _____ (start) doing our school project for tomorrow.

6) Did you manage to _____ (contact) your landlord?

7) They went to Vermont for a weekend. They needed to _____ (escape) the chaos of the city.

8) After years of marriage, Mary managed to _____ (make understand) her husband how to fold t-shirts correctly.

Exercise 7.6

Put the correct preposition or particle next to the verb "GET", choosing among: RID OF (x2), ON/ALONG, OVER, AWAY WITH, AWAY FROM, DOWN TO, THROUGH, THROUGH TO, ACROSS TO.

1) We can't get _____ our neighbor that he shouldn't start the car for an hour before leaving. It's bad for the environment.

2) I should get _____ all my notes and notebooks from my school years. They are cluttering my room, and I don't need them any more.

3) Andrew got _____ studying for the final test one week before the end and got _____ quite well, all things considered.

4) Now that we are abroad our credit cards have been blocked, but we can't get _____ our bank.

5) Our three-month old dog chewed on a book that I had borrowed from the school library, but it got _____ it. After that, I had to get _____ the damaged book and buy a new one for the school library.

6) Every once in a while, we all need to get _____ the grinding routine and do something fun.

7) Do you get _____ with your co-workers?

8) We should get _____ our past disagreements, and start afresh.

Exercise 7.7

Complete the sentences with the following phrasal verbs:
Drop in, Drop out, Help out, Come down on, Call in, Talk (sb) out, Go through, Be in.

1) Yesterday, my nephew _____ (visited) for a visit. He told me he had passed his exam with flying colors!

2) Our secretary has _____ (used the phone) sick today. Would you like to leave a message?

3) Paul _____ (had trouble) a difficult period when he lost his job. Fortunately, he found a better paying job, even closer to home.

4) The manager _____ (rebuked) the crew quite harshly for making some mistakes. A

supervisor should _____ him _____ (convince against) of such bad manners, which can be counterproductive for team-building.

5) After _____ (leaving) of school when he was very young, Mark understood the value of education and got his school degree as an adult.

6) A: Is Laura going to _____ us _____ (help) with the moving on Sunday?
   B: Yes, she said she _____ (join).

Exercise 7.8

Complete the text with the following phrasal verbs:

Drop in, Drop out, Help out, Come down on, Call in, Talk (sb) out, Go through, Be in.

A) Hi! I just 1) _____ briefly to tell you that after the coach 2) _____ Sara so heavily for missing the ball at the match, she has been 3) _____ a tough period. Last week she 4) _____ sick, and now she says that she wants to 5) _____ of the volleyball team. It's a pity because Sara is one of our best players. She is extremely talented, and she really might have a bright future. I want to try and 6) _____ her _____ of her decision. Can you 7) _____ me _____?
B) Yes! I 8) _____ ! You can count on me!

Exercise 7.9

Complete the sentences using: Phrasal Verbs with GET + RID OF, ON/ALONG, OVER, AWAY WITH, AWAY FROM, THROUGH, THROUGH TO, DOWN TO, and _Drop in, Drop out, Help out, Come down on, Call in, Talk (sb) out, Go through, Be in._

1) Two years ago, Nicole _____ a difficult period with her thyroid. She often had to _____ sick because she didn't feel well. Fortunately, the doctors prescribed her a cure which helped her to _____ these problems.

2) The famous artist _____ on his assistant for apparently no reason. Then he decided to _____ all of his paintings and burn them. Fortunately, the assistant managed to _____ him _____ of that. Such is the life of an artist. And of an artist's assistant.

3) Paulette is no longer attending singing classes. She _____. Now she's interested in painting.

CHAPTER 7: DROP/GET — A TEMPEST IN A TEAPOT

4) Could you _____ our boss and tell him that the client he was waiting for has arrived? Thank you.

5) We _____ studying really hard only a few days before the test, and luckily we _____.

6) Your sister _____ the other day and gave me this for you. It's wonderful how you two _____ so well.

7) A magpie stole my earrings from the window, and of course _____ it. I was never able to find them again.

8) We really needed to _____ the daily grind. We thoroughly enjoyed our short vacation.

9) A: We would like to go to the movie theater next Sunday. _____ you _____ ?
   B: Sure, thank you.

10) You can't do everything on your own. You need someone to _____ you _____ .

Exercise 7.10

Look at Text 1 and write these sentences using an idiom, a phrase, or a collocation:

PASS WITH FLYING COLORS	A STORM IS BREWING (x2)	SEE EYE TO EYE
A BRIGHT YOUNG THING	A TEMPEST IN A TEAPOT	MAKE ONE'S BLOOD BOIL
HEAVY-HEARTED	STORM AT SB	BE IN
NOT BELIEVE ONE'S EARS	JOIN FORCES	

1) When Mark told me that he had passed his test with an excellent score, I could hardly believe him. I didn't know he was such a good student.

   _____

   _____

2) I certainly don't agree with people who tend to overreact with you over the smallest thing.

   _____

   _____

3) Tom is <u>extremely sad</u> after breaking up with his girlfriend. He is usually such <u>a cheerful and enthusiastic young man</u>! Let's <u>work together</u> to cheer him up!

_____

_____

4) Look at the sky! It looks really menacing with those big dark clouds... <u>a storm is about to arrive...</u>

_____

_____

5) According to historians, European leaders should have been able to tell that <u>something more dangerous was going to happen</u> when Hitler invaded Poland.

_____

_____

6) Jenny is fine, now. It was all just <u>a big fuss about nothing.</u>

_____

_____

7) The story on the news about a poor dog being abandoned by its family <u>made Paul feel extremely angry and indignant.</u>

_____

_____

8) If you want to go to the movie theater on Saturday, <u>you can count on me</u>! Definitely!

_____

_____

CHAPTER 8: GO — A PASSION FOR HORSES

Text 1 🎧 15

Diane Crump, born in 1948 in Connecticut (USA), was the first woman to ride in a professional horse race in the United States.

She got the idea of applying for her jockey license (license to be a professional horse-rider) in 1968, following the example of another woman, who unfortunately got injured, and soon had to retire. Many male jockeys, trainers, and owners bitterly went on at her and any other woman trying to take up professional horse-riding, and on many occasions really crossed the line with aggressive behavior. In some cases, they even threw rocks at the trailer used as a changing room by the women.

In 1969, a little glimmer of hope appeared when Diane Crump went in for her first race in Florida. On that occasion, the track officials, having noticed such episodes of disrespect, went over the details of the case, and threatened to sanction the male jockeys.

There was a big uproar in the public. It was as if a bomb went off. After the race, as she went out of the changing room, crowds surrounded her with some people shouting, "Go back to the kitchen!"

In 1970, she was the first female jockey to ride in the Kentucky Derby, a very important horse-racing competition.

For many years, the male jockeys went after her to try and make her go back on her decision, putting her in a tough spot on more than one occasion.

Nevertheless, she went on and faced the music with passion and courage. Eventually, such hostility went down. Now it's perfectly normal and acceptable

Text 2 🎧 16

Diane Crump, born in 1948 in Connecticut (USA), was the first woman to ride in a professional horse race in the United States.

She was inspired to apply for her jockey license (license to be a professional horse-rider) in 1968, following the example of another woman, who unfortunately got injured, and soon had to retire. Many male jockeys, trainers, and owners bitterly and repeatedly criticized her and any other woman trying to pursue professional horse-riding, and on many occasions really exaggerated with a display of aggressive behavior.

In some cases, they even threw rocks at the trailer used as a changing room by the women. In 1969, a little sign of improvement appeared, when Diane Crump undertook her first race in Florida. On that occasion, the track officials, having noticed such episodes of disrespect, examined the details of the case, and threatened to sanction the male jockeys.

There was a big uproar in the public. It was as if a bomb exploded. After the race, as she exited the changing room, crowds surrounded her with some people shouting, "Return to the kitchen!" In 1970, she was the first female jockey to ride in the Kentucky Derby, a very important horse-racing competition.

For many years, the male jockeys chased her to try and make her change her mind, putting her in difficult situations on more than one occasion.

Nevertheless, she continued on and faced the consequences of her choice with passion and courage.

for a western woman to pursue a career in horse-riding. But it wouldn't have been possible without the contribution of Diane Crump and all the other women who <u>went off the beaten path</u> and changed a little bit of history.

Eventually, such hostility <u>diminished</u>. Now it is perfectly normal and acceptable for a western woman to pursue a career in horse-riding. However, it would not have been possible without the contribution of Diane Crump and all the other women who <u>stepped out of the conventional path</u> and changed a little portion of history.

Text readapted from Wikipedia

Vocabulary:

Go on at (sb) (phrasal verb) (BrE) = _____

Take up (a new interest) (phrasal verb) =

_____

Cross the line (idiom) = _____

A glimmer of hope (collocation) = _____

Go in for (sth) (phrasal verb) = _____

Go over (sth) (phrasal verb) = _____

Go off (phrasal verb) = _____

Go out of (a place) (phrasal verb) = _____

Go back (phrasal verb) = _____

Go after (sb) (phrasal verb) = _____

Go back on (a decision, a choice) (phrasal verb) =

_____

Put sb/ Be in a tough spot (idiom) = _____

Go on (phrasal verb) = _____

Face the music (idiom) = _____

Go down (phrasal verb) = _____

Go off the beaten path (idiom) = _____

Exercise 8.1 🎧 15

Listen to text n. 1 while following along from text 2.

Exercise 8.2 🎧 16

Listen to text n. 2 while following along from text 1.

Exercise 8.3

Read the two texts, and complete the phrasal verbs and idiomatic expressions with their meaning.

Exercise 8.4

Listen to text n. 1 again, press pause after each sentence, and repeat.

Exercise 8.5

Put the correct preposition or particle next to the verb "GO", choosing among: ON, ON AT, BACK, OFF, OVER, DOWN, AFTER, IN FOR, OUT OF, BACK ON.

GO ON	GO OFF	GO AFTER	GO OUT OF
GO ON AT	GO OVER	GO IN FOR	GO BACK ON
GO BACK	GO DOWN		

1) The teacher _____ (examined) Mike's essay, and gave him some suggestions on how to improve some points.

2) Prices of gas have _____ (decreased) again, fortunately.

3) During the fire, lots of power generators _____ (exploded), making it more difficult for the firefighters to put out the fire.

4) Please, don't get distracted. _____ (continue) with what you're doing.

5) When she _____ (exited) the store, it was raining.

6) Many people in the office had been _____ ing _____ (criticize) the new manager's decisions, but she didn't _____ (change her mind) her decisions.

7) After many years of work, Mike has decided to _____ (return) to college and _____ (undertake) another career.

8) Our cat is incredible at _____ ing _____ (chasing) mice.

Exercise 8.6

Put the correct preposition or particle next to the verb "GO", choosing among: ON, ON AT, BACK, OFF, OVER, DOWN, AFTER, IN FOR, OUT OF, BACK ON.

1) In certain parts of Africa, it is dangerous to walk in fields because a hidden mine might go _____.

2) Liz always went _____ her younger brother for never helping her out with the housework.

3) Once we went _____ the house, we realized that the temperature had drastically gone _____. So, we had to go _____ in to get our coats.

4) The manager would like to go _____ the details of your project.

5) Kate never went _____ her promises, but in that case, she probably simply forgot all about it.

6) He listened to what she had to say, and then he went _____ with what he was doing.

7) I saw Mary crying and running away, so I went _____ her to try and cheer her up.

8) Is Mark going to go _____ the marathon?

Exercise 8.7

Complete the sentences with the following phrasal verbs in the correct tense:
Go in for, Go on, Go on at, Go down, Go over, Go after, Go out of, Go back, Go back on, Take up (x2).

1) Mary originally _____ wrestling, but after the first lesson she _____ her decision and _____ something else.

2) I wonder if prices will ever _____ . We cannot _____ like this much longer.

3) Sabrina has _____ a drama course, and she is learning to _____ her comfort zone.

4) The editor _____ the translation. Although he found some major mistakes, he did not _____ the translator, but made some polite suggestions.

5) The hounds _____ the fox, but fortunately they did not catch it.

6) Once Mike moved to New York, he seldom had time to _____ to his home town to visit his family. Only at Christmas.

Exercise 8.8

Complete the story with the following phrasal verbs in the correct tense: *Go in for, Go on, Go on at, Go down, Go over, Go after, Go out of, Go back, Go back on, Take up.*

When Jack 1) _____ drama, he did not realize what he was 2) _____ . He was not used to 3) _____ his own promises, so he decided to 4) _____ with the classes. One day, the teacher asked him to throw himself on the floor and pretend that a predator was 5) _____ him. Jack was utterly embarrassed, and for a moment he thought of never 6) _____ again, but then he did it. He managed to 7) _____ his comfort zone and from that day on, his concerns about other people's opinion 8) _____ considerably. In the end, he was assigned a part in the play. As soon as he was given the script, he zealously 9) _____ it, and studied it in great detail. He was determined to make a great performance.

Exercise 8.9

Look at Text 1 and write these sentences using an idiom, a phrase, or a collocation:

CROSS THE LINE	PUT SB IN A TOUGH SPOT
A GLIMMER OF HOPE	GO OFF THE BEATEN PATH
FACE THE MUSIC	

1) My grandfather always told me that I should have the courage to <u>do something different than everyone else.</u>

   _____

   _____

2) It is not nice to <u>put someone else in difficulty.</u> One should always try their best to make people feel at ease.

   _____

   _____

3) They really <u>behaved disrespectfully</u>. Now they are going to face the <u>consequences of their actions</u>.

_____

_____ <u>for their actions.</u>

4) I thought I had miserably failed the test, but then going over it with my classmates, I started to have <u>a little bit of hope</u>.

_____

_____

CHAPTER 9: HAND/KEEP — PUT YOUR THINKING CAP ON!

Text 1 🎧 17

There she was, sitting at her classroom desk, feeling on edge, waiting for her teacher to hand out the blank sheets for the essay. It was the end of term. Laura didn't want to be kept back that year, and had been trying to ace all the final tests.

She was feeling so nervous that she was starting to well up with tears, but she managed to keep them in.

The atmosphere was so tense that you could cut the air with a knife. The teacher became aware of it, so she asked everyone to take three big breaths, with the idea of breathing positive energy in, and breathing all the tension out.

The students let out some laughter, but the teacher asked to keep the noise down. Then she gave them instructions to complete the test and asked to keep to them. She also reminded them that they had to keep off any external sources, such as the internet.

Finally, she advised the students to keep up with the assigned time so as to be able to hand in the test thoroughly completed and double-checked.

She wished them luck and said they could now get started. Laura put on her thinking cap, determined to do her best.

Although it felt more like a race against time, she kept on writing and she even had enough time to go over her text again.

It turned out that Laura had really nailed it with that final essay. The cherry on top was that she also carried off successfully all the other final tests, revealing a very bright mind. From then on, she

Text 2 🎧 18

There she was, sitting at her classroom desk, feeling terribly nervous, waiting for her teacher to distribute the blank sheets for the essay. It was the end of term. Laura did not wish to be held back a school year, and had been trying to pass with a high score all the final tests.

She was feeling so nervous that her eyes started to fill with tears, but she managed to restrain herself.

The atmosphere was so tense that you could tangibly feel it. The teacher became aware of it, so she asked everyone to take three big breaths, with the idea of inhaling positive energy, and exhaling all the tension.

The students let out some laughter, but the teacher asked them to be quiet. Then she gave them instructions to complete the test and asked to follow them. She also reminded them that they had to avoid any external sources, such as the internet.

Finally, she advised the students to keep pace with the assigned time so as to be able to give her the test thoroughly completed and double-checked.

She wished them luck and said they could now begin. Laura started to think about the assignment seriously and with focus, determined to do her best.

Although it felt like she did not have enough time, she continued writing and she even had enough time to check her text again.

It unexpectedly happened that Laura did really well with that final essay. On top of that, she also passed successfully all the other final tests, revealing a very bright mind.

learned to believe in herself and in her resources. She never <u>fell behind with</u> school assignments and she learned to <u>run things like clockwork</u>.

From then on, she learned to believe in herself and in her resources. She never <u>failed to meet</u> the school assignment <u>requirements</u> and she learned to <u>manage things in a timely, and well organized manner</u>.

Vocabulary:

Feel on edge (idiom) = _____

Hand (sth) out (phrasal verb) = _____

Be kept back (phrasal verb) (AmE)= _____

Ace a test/ a job interview (idiom) = _____

Well up with tears (idiom) = _____

Keep (sth) in (phrasal verb) = _____

Cut the air with a knife (idiom) = _____

Breathe (sth) in (phrasal verb) = _____

Breathe (sth) out (phrasal verb) = _____

Keep (sth) down (phrasal verb) = _____

Keep to (sth) (phrasal verb) = _____

Keep off (sth) (phrasal verb) = _____

Keep up with (sth) (phrasal verb) = _____

Hand (sth) in (phrasal verb) = _____

Get started (phrase) = _____

Put on one's thinking cap (idiom) = _____

A race against time (idiom) = _____

Keep on (+ing) (phrasal verb) = _____

Turn out (phrasal verb) = _____

Nail something (idiom) = _____

The cherry on top (AmE) / The cherry on top of the cake (BrE) (idiom) = _____

Carry sth off (phrasal verb) = _____

Fall behind with (sth) (phrasal verb) = _____

Run things like clockwork (idiom) = _____

Exercise 9.1 🎧 17

Listen to text n. 1 while following along from text 2.

Exercise 9.2 🎧 18

Listen to text n. 2 while following along from text 1.

Exercise 9.3

Read the two texts, and complete the phrasal verbs and idiomatic expressions with their meaning.

Exercise 9.4

Listen to text n. 1 again, press pause after each sentence, and repeat.

Exercise 9.5

Put the correct preposition or particle next to the verb "KEEP", choosing among: ON, BACK, OFF, DOWN, TO, UP WITH, IN.

KEEP ON	KEEP OFF	KEEP UP WITH	KEEP IN
KEEP BACK	KEEP DOWN	KEEP TO	

1) Tom and Paul went jogging together, but Paul couldn't _____ (keep pace) Tom because he was too fast.

2) _____ (stay away from) the grass, please.

3) He carefully read the instructions, and he did his best to _____ (follow) them.

4) Unfortunately, Mark didn't study hard, and he was _____ (to be held back) one school year.

5) The teacher asked the students to _____ the noise _____ (quiet down), and he _____ (continued) explaining the new topic.

6) She is the type of person who _____ everything _____ (not talk) when she has a problem.

Exercise 9.6

Put the correct preposition or particle next to the verb "KEEP", choosing among: ON, BACK, OFF, DOWN, TO, UP WITH, IN.

1) Please children, keep it _____. Your baby brother is sleeping.

2) Little Red Riding Hood didn't keep _____ what her mother had told her, and took the shortcut through the woods. When she met the wolf, she didn't keep _____ walking, but she stopped to pick up some flowers. After her adventure, she understood that she had to keep _____ the dangerous path. (From the fairy tale "Little Red Riding Hood")

3) If a student doesn't study hard and gets bad grades, he is kept _____ one year.

4) Life is sometimes chaotic, and it becomes difficult to keep _____ all the things to do. When it happens, one shouldn't keep everything _____ and feel overwhelmed, but ask for help.

Exercise 9.7

Complete the sentences with the following phrasal verbs:
Hand out, Breathe in, Breathe out, Hand in, Fall behind with, Turn out.

1) He found a summer job. Nothing complicated. He just has to _____ (give) flyers to the passersby.

2) Jack wondered why the power in his house had been cut off. It _____ (happen) that he had _____ (fail to meet) the payments of the electricity bills.

3) For this exercise, you have to _____ (inhale) slowly, hold your breath in for a few seconds, and _____ the air _____ (exhale) as if you were blowing out a candle.

4) Have you _____ (given) your assignment to the teacher? No, not yet.

Exercise 9.8

Complete the text with the following phrasal verbs:
Hand out, Breathe in, Breathe out, Hand in, Fall behind with, Turn out.

When the teacher 1) _____ the test, James gasped in disappointment. Most of the test was about the topic he had 2) _____ . He was perfectly ready in the other topic, but not this one. He deeply 3) _____ , and then 4) _____ , trying to remember as much as he could. When he finally 5) _____ the test to the teacher, he wasn't sure of a couple of details. It 6) _____ that he got most of the answers correct and he got a very good grade.

Exercise 9.10

Complete the sentences using: Phrasal Verbs with KEEP + ON, BACK,

OFF, DOWN, TO, UP WITH, IN and Hand out, Breathe in, Breathe out, Hand in, Fall behind with, Turn out.

1) If you are feeling anxious, _____ and _____, until you feel more relaxed.

2) Jack doesn't like doing math with his brother. He _____ talking, and showing him the procedures quickly, and Jack can't _____ him.

3) _____ the flower bed, children! I just planted the flowers!

4) Children, please _____ the volume of the TV _____, or you will disturb the neighbors.

5) When the teacher _____ the test results, Brenda had a pleasant surprise. She was on
cloud nine from happiness, but she _____ everything _____ because it _____
that her best friend had got a terrible grade, instead.

6) During mid-term, Mark _____ terribly _____ the tests and assignments. It was a miracle
he wasn't _____ that year.

Exercise 9.11

Look at Text 1 and write these sentences using an idiom, a phrase, or a collocation:

FEEL ON EDGE	PUT ON ONE'S THINKING CAP
ACE A TEST/JOB INTERVIEW	THE CHERRY ON TOP
WELL UP WITH TEARS	RUN THINGS LIKE CLOCKWORK
CUT THE AIR WITH A KNIFE	NAIL SOMETHING
GET STARTED	RACE AGAINST TIME

1) Oooh, that hot chocolate on such a cold day really gave me what I needed! And the whipped cream was really the best of the best!

_____

_____

2) Come on! Think hard! We need a solution!

_____

3) I'm sorry to interrupt you, but we should really begin.

_____

4) My sister is extremely well-organized!

_____

5) I knew you would start crying watching this film...

_____

_____

6) The tension in the room was tangible. You could really feel it!

_____

_____

7) Sally felt extremely nervous for the driving test, but in the end she did everything correctly, and she passed.

_____

_____

8) We were terribly late, and the traffic was unbelievable. We tried our hardest to catch the last train! Fortunately, we managed to take it!

_____

_____

CHAPTER 10: LOOK — 3000

Text 1 🎧 19

Looking back on her childhood, 1000 years before, Anne was pleased to see how things had changed. First of all, amazing advancements in the removal of radiation from food and water had been made. Second, they were starting to see the connections between de-ionized food and longevity.

Sure, there was still a lot to work on, but at least, it was no longer the time when people looked down on each other if they spotted any differences.

At this point, it didn't really matter any more. Not after the massive atomic bomb had blown up.

She looked on everyone in her crew as a good friend, and she was sure her warm feelings were mutual.

Life wasn't always a piece of cake in The Pod, and they still had to look out for danger when they left the base. When they ventured on an expedition, they still had to look out for edible food, but this was no longer a reason for division, like in her tender age. On the contrary, it boosted a sense of community and belonging, which had been abandoned by society when she was a child. Now, the victory of a member of the crew was genuinely looked on as an accomplishment of the whole community. No more green with envy, please.

Captain Anne DuChant really felt the human race was finally at a turning point.

1000 years had passed by. There hadn't been a single day that Anne hadn't checked the atmosphere data, and only now, at last, the levels of carbon dioxide and uranium on Planet Earth were starting to go down. Would it ever be possible to live outside

Text 2 🎧 20

Remembering her childhood, 1000 years before, Anne was pleased to see how things had changed. First of all, amazing advancements in the removal of radiation from food and water had been made. Secondly, they were starting to see the connections between de-ionized food and longevity.

Certainly, there was still a lot to work on, but at least it was no longer the time when people treated each other poorly if they detected any differences.

At this point, this was not a matter of concern any more. Not after the massive atomic bomb had exploded.

She regarded everyone in her crew as a good friend, and she was sure her warm feelings were reciprocated.

Life was not always easy in The Pod, and they still had to beware of danger when they left the base. When they ventured on an expedition, they still had to pay attention to see if they could find edible food, but this was no longer a reason for division, like in her younger years. On the contrary, it enhanced a sense of community and belonging, which had been abandoned by society when she was a child. Now, the victory of a member of the crew was genuinely seen as an accomplishment of the whole community. No more envy, please.

Captain Anne DuChant really felt the human race was finally at a time of decisive change.

1000 years had elapsed. There had not been a single day that Anne had not checked the atmosphere data, and only now, at last, the levels of carbon

The Pod again? Would humanity ever be "the salt of the earth"?

An unusual beeping interrupted her train of thought. She looked the data over. A value caught her eye... What did it mean? She had never seen it before.

She had her AI assistant look through all the sources available. It took Anne and her team days to figure out what it meant and how to weigh all the pros and cons.

The crew was in a tight spot. Was it really time to leave The Pod? Was it realistically safe? It was the year 3000. They had escaped extinction for 1000 years, and now they couldn't afford to risk the young ones' lives.

Anne was especially torn. On the one hand, she truly looked forward to recreating the landscapes of her school years; on the other hand, she was fully aware of what was at stake. What would you do in this situation?

Would you jump right in or gradually phase in?

dioxide and uranium on Planet Earth were starting to decrease. Would it ever be possible to live outside The Pod again? Would humanity ever be made up of good and honest people?

An unusual beeping interrupted her thoughts. She examined the data quickly, almost distractedly. A value caught her attention... What did it mean? She had never seen it before.

She had her AI assistant search all the sources available. It took Anne and her team days to understand what it meant and how to ponder all the positive and bad aspects of it.

The crew was called to make a difficult decision. Was it really time to leave The Pod? Was it realistically safe? It was the year 3000. They had escaped extinction for 1000 years, and now they could not afford to risk the young ones' lives.

Anne was especially undecided. On the one hand, she truly had been waiting in anticipation of recreating the landscapes of her school years; on the other hand, she was fully aware of what there was to lose.

What would you do in this situation? Would you take action enthusiastically and almost hastily or introduce yourself to this new phase in gradual stages?

Vocabulary:

Look back on (sth) (phrasal verb) = _____

Look down on (sth/sb) (phrasal verb) = _____

Blow (sth) up (phrasal verb) = _____

Look on (sth/sb) (phrasal verb) = _____

It's a piece of cake (idiom) = _____

Look out (phrasal verb) = _____

Look out for (sth/sb) = _____

Tender age (collocation) = _____

(Be) Green with envy (idiom) = _____

(Be) at a turning point (phrase) = _____

Pass by/ Go by (phrasal verb) = _____

Go down (phrasal verb) = _____

Be the salt of the earth (idiom) = _____

Train of thought (phrase) = _____

Look (sth) over (phrasal verb) = _____

Catch one's eye (idiom) = _____

Look through (sth) (phrasal verb) = _____

Figure (sth) out (phrasal verb) = _____

Weigh all the pros and cons (phrase) =

_____

Be in a tight spot (idiom) = _____

Be torn (idiom) = _____

Look forward to (sth) (phrasal verb) =

_____

Be at stake (idiom) = _____

Jump in (phrasal verb) = _____

Phase in (phrasal verb) = _____

Exercise 10.1 🎧 19

Listen to text n. 1 while following along from text 2.

Exercise 10.2 🎧 20

Listen to text n. 2 while following along from text 1.

Exercise 10.3

Read the two texts, and complete the phrasal verbs and idiomatic expressions with their meaning.

Exercise 10.4

Listen to text n. 1 again, press pause after each sentence, and repeat.

Exercise 10.5

Put the correct preposition or particle next to the verb "LOOK", choosing among: BACK ON, DOWN ON, ON, OUT, OUT FOR, OVER, THROUGH, FORWARD TO.

LOOK BACK ON,	LOOK OUT	LOOK THROUGH
LOOK DOWN ON	LOOK OUT FOR	LOOK FORWARD TO
LOOK ON	LOOK OVER	

1) Deborah has a very high opinion of herself. She's always _____ (treating badly) anyone who thinks differently than her.

2) _____ (Be careful)! You're going to fall!

3) Mark _____ (checked distractingly) the pile of unread mail.

4) _____ (try and find) a blue house with a white door. That's Jill's house.

5) Whenever he _____ (remembered) his school years, a hint of a smile appeared on his face.

6) Mark _____ (searched) all his unread mail, but he couldn't find the unpaid bill.

7) Matt was _____ (waiting in anticipation) going to the concert.

8) Whenever the school principal entered a classroom, he was _____ (regarded/ considered) with a mixture of fear and respect.

Exercise 10.6

Put the correct preposition or particle next to the verb "LOOK", choosing among: BACK ON, DOWN ON, ON, OUT, OUT FOR, OVER, THROUGH, FORWARD TO.

1) Sylvie used to look _____ people who enjoy spending time outdoors in nature, but now she's coming round to a different opinion.

2) They've always looked _____ her as a family member even if she was just a friend.

3) Looking _____ those days, it appears clear that selling that house was a mistake.

4) During his job interview, the HR manager looked _____ his education and went straight to the job experience part.

5) Look _____ when you are traveling alone. You need to be more vigilant than in normal conditions.

6) I have looked _____ all my coats and jackets, but I can't find my keys.

7) Look _____ a little lady with red hair and a white dog when you arrive at the airport. That's your host mother.

8) We are looking _____ receiving your prompt reply.

Exercise 10.7

Complete the sentences with the following phrasal verbs: *Blow up, Pass by/Go by, Go down, Figure out, Jump into, Phase in.*

1) The experts are still trying to _____ (understand) what caused the generator to _____ (explode) and catch fire.

2) It's rather typical of him to _____ (take action over-enthusiastically) with both feet _____ a new business without thinking carefully enough.

3) Time _____(elapsed), and no one remembered it any more.

4) The company gradually phased the old machinery out, and carefully _____ the new ones _____ (gradually introduced).

5) In September, temperatures _____ (decrease) considerably, especially at night and in the morning.

Exercise 10.8

Complete the text with the following phrasal verbs: *Blow up, Pass by/Go by, Go down, Figure out, Jump in, Phase in.*

After the electric generator 1) _____, it took months to 2) _____ before the engineers could 3) _____ the causes of the explosion. Some components of the team wanted to 4) _____ and just solve the problem as soon as possible, also taking advantage of the fact that the price of the generators had 5) _____ in that period. The majority of the team, however, tried to gradually 6) _____ new solutions _____ to observe what worked best.

Exercise 10.9

Complete the sentences using: Phrasal Verbs with LOOK + BACK ON, DOWN ON, ON, OUT, OUT FOR, OVER, THROUGH, FORWARD TO and *Blow up, Pass by/Go by, Go down, Figure out, Jump into, Phase in.*

1) _____! A house just caught fire and the wires might _____. Quick! Let's call the firefighters!

2) They _____ all their records, and finally they found the document they had been looking for.

3) They often _____ the years of their youth and thought they had had a wonderful life together.

4) I used to _____ smartphones, but then I had to buy one.

5) He _____ the text, but his mind was somewhere else.

6) When we go downtown, _____ bargains. Prices have _____ this week.

7) If you dress too extravagantly in some countries, people might _____ you with a little bit of suspicion and perplexity.

8) Before _____ a new business project, let's try to _____ what the real profit margin would be.

9) The baby was gradually _____ to different flavors and solid foods.

10) It's incredible how fast time _____ when you are having fun!

11) We are really _____ seeing you! When are you coming to visit us?

CHAPTER 10: LOOK — 3000

Exercise 10.10

Look at Text 1 and write these sentences using an idiom, a phrase, or a collocation:

IT'S A PIECE OF CAKE   TRAIN OF THOUGHT

TENDER AGE   CATCH ONE'S EYE

GREEN WITH ENVY   WEIGH THE PROS AND CONS

BE AT A TURNING POINT   BE IN A TIGHT SPOT

BE AT STAKE   BE TORN

BE THE SALT OF THE EARTH

1) Jasmine is <u>a really good and honest person</u>!

2) I know you are <u>faced with a difficult decision</u> right now. It's understandable that you are <u>undecided</u> between these two choices. All you need to do is sit down and <u>ponder carefully the advantages and disadvantages</u> of each. Then making up your mind will be <u>extremely easy</u>!

3) We need to take action now. The life of our planet is <u>at risk.</u>

4) American actress Shirley Temple began her career at the <u>young age</u> of three.

69

5) She realized that <u>it was a pivotal moment of change</u> in her career.

_____

_____

6) The stepsisters became <u>very envious</u> when they found out that the crystal shoe fit Cinderella's foot perfectly. (From the fairy tale "Cinderella")

_____

_____

7) A glimpse in the distance <u>caught her attention</u> and she lost her <u>concentration</u>.

_____

_____

CHAPTER 11: MAKE — A TRIP DOWN MEMORY LANE

Text 1 🎧 21

After years of saving up, they had finally made it! Mike and his friends, a group made up of three bold young men and four young ladies in their twenties, had landed in Rome and were determined to have the time of their life!

Three days in majestic Rome, three days in wonderful Florence, a detour to central Italy — Mike's place of origin — and then to Venice, all in the scorching sun of August, driving a rented van.

The atmosphere was electric. Everyone was on cloud nine. It wasn't hard to guess what they had made of the country so far! They just loved every minute!

Mike himself was totally thrilled by the idea of going back to the places of his childhood. He had been more fun than ever during this trip: always cracking a joke and making everyone roar with laughter.

It was when they actually arrived in Moresco, an enchanting medieval town in central Italy, that he started to grow silent. As soon as they got to the bed & breakfast, he mumbled something and made straight for the main square.Nobody could make out what he said, but they didn't put too much thought into it. The next day, though, when everyone was ready to hop in the van, he made up an excuse and stayed in town.

A magnetic force was driving him through these secluded alleys. This town seemed to stir up memories that he had long forgotten...

He remembered somewhere around here, there was his grandfather's house... the house where he

Text 2 🎧 22

After years of setting money aside, they had finally made it! Mike and his friends, a group composed of three bold young men and four young ladies in their twenties, had landed in Rome and were determined to have a lot of fun!

Three days in majestic Rome, three days in wonderful Florence, a detour to central Italy — Mike's place of origin — and then to Venice, all in the scorching sun of August, driving a rented van.

The atmosphere was electric. Everyone was elated. It was not hard to guess what opinion they had formed of the country so far! They just loved every minute!

Mike himself was totally thrilled by the idea of going back to the places of his childhood. He had been more fun than ever during this trip: always telling a joke and making everyone laugh heartily.

It was when they actually arrived in Moresco, an enchanting medieval town in central Italy, that he started to grow silent. As soon as they arrived at the bed & breakfast, he mumbled something and went into the direction of the main square.

Nobody could understand what he said, but they did not pay too much attention to it. The next day, though, when everyone was ready to go into the van, he invented an excuse and stayed in town.

A magnetic force was driving him through these secluded alleys. This town seemed to stir up memories that he had long forgotten...

He remembered somewhere around here, there was his grandfather's house... the house where he had spent so many happy summers. Where was it? Was it this way, or was it that way?

Suddenly, he saw it! <u>Memories came flooding back!</u> Good ones, like all the times he had played chess with his grandfather, and bad ones, like towards the end, when he had found him <u>passed out</u> in the kitchen, and how, sadly, three days later he had <u>passed away</u> in the hospital.

That had been the last summer he had spent here. How sweet it was to be in this town again. <u>Out of the blue</u>, a hand touched his shoulder. He turned around: Jill, his best friend, was standing beside him.

"Are you ok, Mike? You've been <u>acting weird</u> these days... You're <u>looking blue</u>, so the girls and I have even <u>made up a song</u> to <u>cheer you up!</u>"

Mike told her about his sudden <u>rush of memories</u>. Jill understood him immediately. She suggested that he should <u>take it easy</u> for the next couple of days.

The following day, Mike and Jill went on a walk, tracing back Mike's grandfather's favorite path, and played chess. Mike was delighted to share his recollections with Jill. It felt as if by doing so, he could <u>make up with</u> this long buried part of his life. He was grateful to have such a caring friend as Jill. When he was ready, they came back to the bed & breakfast. The others had been cooling off in the swimming pool.

When they arrived, the boys started teasing him. "At last! The only good thing to <u>make up for</u> your awkwardness has been this swimming pool! Are you doing ok?"

"Yes, I'm sorry, guys. I'm <u>as good as new</u>, now!"

had spent so many happy summers. Where was it? Was it this way, or was it that way?

Suddenly, he saw it! <u>Memories came back to his mind!</u> Good ones, like all the times he had played chess with his grandfather, and bad ones, like towards the end, when he had found him <u>fainted</u> in the kitchen, and how, sadly, three days later he had <u>died</u> in the hospital.

That had been the last summer he had spent here. How sweet it was to be in this town again. <u>All of a sudden</u>, a hand touched his shoulder. He turned around: Jill, his best friend, was standing beside him.

"Are you ok, Mike? You've been <u>behaving differently</u> than usual these days... You're <u>looking sad</u>, so the girls and I have even <u>created a song</u> to <u>make you happy again!</u>"

Mike told her about his <u>sudden powerful recollection of memories</u>. Jill understood him immediately. She suggested that he should <u>relax</u> for the next couple of days.

The following day, Mike and Jill went on a walk, tracing back Mike's grandfather's favorite path, and played chess. Mike was delighted to share his recollections with Jill. He felt as if by doing so, he could <u>make peace</u> with this long buried part of his life. He was grateful to have such a caring friend as Jill. When he was ready, they came back to the bed & breakfast. The others had been <u>refreshing themselves</u> in the swimming pool.

When they arrived, the boys started teasing him. "At last! The only good thing to <u>compensate for</u> your awkwardness has been this swimming pool! Are you doing ok?"

"You bet! You're at the wheel tomorrow!"

"All right, to make it up to you guys, I'm going to treat you to a pizza, tonight!"

And that's how a trip down memory lane restored Mike's sense of identity and gave him a new sense of purpose in life.

Yes, I'm sorry, guys. I'm in very good condition, now!"

"You bet! You're driving tomorrow!"

"All right, to compensate for my bad behavior, I'm going to buy you a pizza, tonight!"

And that is how this time spent recollecting past memories restored Mike's sense of identity and gave him a new sense of purpose in life.

Vocabulary:

Save (sth) up (phrasal verb) = _____

Be made up of (phrasal verb) = _____

Have the time of one's life (idiom) = _____

Be on cloud nine (idiom) = _____

Make of (sth) (phrasal verb) = _____

Crack jokes (idiom) = _____

Roar with laughter (collocation) = _____

Make for (phrasal verb) = _____

Make (sth/sb) out (phrasal verb) = _____

Not put much thought into something (phrase) = _____

Make (sth) up (1) (phrasal verb) = _____

Memories came flooding back (phrase) = _____

Pass out (phrasal verb) = _____

Pass away (phrasal verb) = _____

Out of the blue (idiom) = _____

Act weird (phrase) = _____

Look/ be/feel blue (idiom) = _____

Make (sth) up (2) (phrasal verb) = _____

Cheer (sb) up (phrasal verb) = _____

Have a rush of memories (phrase) = _____

Take it easy (idiom) = _____

Make up with (sth/sb) (phrasal verb) = _____

Cool (sth/sb) off (phrasal verb) = _____

Make up for (sth) (phrasal verb) = _____

Be as good as new (idiom) = _____

Be at the wheel (idiom) = _____

Make (sth) up (to sb) (phrasal verb) = _____

A trip/ a walk down memory lane (idiom) =

_____

Exercise 11.1 🎧 21

Listen to text n. 1 while following along from text 2.

Exercise 11.2 🎧 22

Listen to text n. 2 while following along from text 1.

Exercise 11.3

Read the two texts, and complete the phrasal verbs and idiomatic expressions with their meaning.

Exercise 11.4

Listen to text n. 1 again, press pause after each sentence, and repeat.

Exercise 11.5

Put the correct preposition or particle next to the verb "MAKE", choosing among: FOR, OF, OUT, UP OF, UP (x2), UP FOR, UP TO, UP WITH.

| MAKE FOR | MAKE OUT | MAKE UP (x2) | MAKE UP TO |
| MAKE OF | MAKE UP OF | MAKE UP FOR | MAKE UP WITH |

1) Our class is _____ (composed of) ten girls and eight boys.

2) Did you see the musical? What did you _____ (think) it?

3) I don't really want to go to the party. I think I'll _____ something _____ (invent) and stay at home that day.

4) To _____ (compensate for) the fact that he couldn't sing, he became an excellent guitar player.

5) He always mumbles when he speaks, and it's very difficult to _____ (understand) what he says.

6) Offended, she _____ (went toward) the door, and left the room.

7) Lauren was so bored that she _____ (created) a song for her cat.

8) Jeff and his sister had an argument, but they soon _____ (made peace) each other.

9) Anne forgot about her sister's birthday. To _____ it _____ (compensate for her bad behavior) her, she bought her two tickets to her favorite concert.

Exercise 11.6

Put the correct preposition or particle next to the verb "MAKE", choosing among: FOR (x2), OF, OUT, UP OF, UP (x2), UP FOR, UP TO (x2), UP WITH

1) As soon as the cat heard its master was awake, it made _____ the kitchen, looking for food.

2) Pinocchio! You shouldn't make _____ lies! You should always tell the truth! (From the children's novel *Pinocchio*, by Carlo Collodi)

3) When Christopher Columbus made _____ the East Indies, his fleet was made _____ three ships.

4) A rapper is a person who can make _____ rhymes and coordinate them to rhythm.

5) We don't know what to make _____ the new manager, yet. Time will tell.

6) Unfortunately, a lady with a giant hat was sitting in front of me at the theater and I couldn't make anything _____ .

7) You should ask for a refund to make _____ the fact that you received faulty goods.

8) Since they sent you faulty goods, the company should issue a refund to make it _____ you.

9) Did Lauren make _____ her boyfriend after his *faux pas*? He should at least buy her dinner to make it _____ her.

Exercise 11.7

Complete the sentences with the following phrasal verbs: *Save up, Pass out, Pass away, Cheer up, Cool off*

1) There's nothing better than a nice swimming pool to _____ (refresh oneself) in summer.

2) When Peter's dog _____ (died), for a while there was nothing that could _____ him _____ (console)

3) The other day, it was so hot and humid that a woman coming out of a restaurant _____ (fainted).

4) After _____ ing _____ for months (setting aside money), Jack and Sarah were able to buy the armchair of their dreams.

Exercise 11.8

Complete the text with the following phrasal verbs: *Save up, Pass out, Pass away, Cheer up, Cool off*.

John was feeling really blue that day... and hot. It was an unbearably boiling summer. Another heat-wave had hit England, and his British house wasn't ready for such high temperature. Nor had been Pinky, his goldfish, who had sadly 1) _____ that day due to the heat. When John had found out, he had nearly 2) _____ . Ironically, he had just finished 3) _____ ing _____ enough money to start the process of insulating the house and finally be able to 4) _____ it _____, and keeping it that way in summer, and warm in winter. That very same day, John called the workers so that they could start the process. However, that evening, to his surprise, he found a new goldfish in the bowl: a gift from his girlfriend to 5) _____ him _____ .

Exercise 11.9

Complete the sentences using: Phrasal Verbs with MAKE + FOR, OF, OUT, UP OF, UP (x2), UP FOR, UP TO, UP WITH and *Save up, Pass out, Pass away, Cheer up, Cool off* (x2).

1) He _____ the door so that he could _____ outside, and enjoy the evening summer breeze.

2) As she _____, someone tried to wet her forehead and wrists to _____ her _____ and help her come round again.

3) Mary ordered a take-away pizza to _____ the fact that she hadn't had time to make dinner that evening.

4) Lauren won't _____ until she _____ her sister. She really hates staying angry for too long.

5) I don't know what to _____ that film. The ending was a little perplexing. Certainly, I didn't expect the main protagonist to _____ ! I suppose it was a rather artistic film.

6) The other day, I _____ an excuse so as to stay at home and watch the open tennis tournament. Maddy found out. Now I need to do something to _____ it _____ her.

7) My son _____ a new game. He's so creative!

8) I didn't _____ how much exactly Mark has _____ for his car so far. However, $100 doesn't sound quite like enough.

9) The building is _____ a central part and two lateral wings.

Exercise 11.10

Look at Text 1 and write these sentences using an idiom, a phrase, or a collocation:

HAVE THE TIME OF ONE'S LIFE	OUT OF THE BLUE
BE ON CLOUD NINE	HAVE A RUSH OF MEMORIES
ACT WEIRD	MEMORIES CAME FLOODING BACK
CRACK JOKES	TAKE IT EASY
ROAR WITH LAUGHTER	BE AS GOOD AS NEW
FEEL BLUE	BE AT THE WHEEL
NOT PUT MUCH THOUGHT INTO SOMETHING	A TRIP DOWN MEMORY LANE

1) John really knows how to relax. Any time we are together, he tells lots of jokes and we all laugh heartily.

_____

_____.

2) Don't <u>feel sad</u> for your dress. Grandma fixed it, and now it <u>looks like new</u>.

_____

_____

3) Soon after getting his driver license, Paul felt <u>elated</u> when his father let him <u>drive</u> for the first time.

_____

_____

4) When I visited my summer home from childhood, the moment I entered <u>memories came back to me</u> <u>all of a sudden</u>.

_____

_____

5) Every time I see that picture, I have <u>lots of memories come back to me</u>.

_____

6) The dinner with my classmates went really well. We really had <u>the best time of our lives</u> with our <u>recollections from the past</u>.

_____

_____

7) Mike is wearing a red sock and a green one. I guess he <u>didn't put too much consideration into</u> his getting dressed today.

_____

_____

8) What's wrong with Paul these days? He's <u>behaving differently than usual</u>.

_____

9) I was having a walk, when <u>all of a sudden</u> a cat appeared in front of my eyes.

_____

CHAPTER 12: PUT — A BUMPY RIDE

Text 1 🎧 23

Peter had felt on top of the world when his architecture studio had won the bid to put up one of the most prestigious skyscrapers in Manhattan in collaboration with the best international architecture studio of all time. He felt this was a once-in-a-lifetime opportunity. In fact, it was. What he hadn't realized was that this was going to be all but smooth sailing. Every time a problem arose, it was indeed like opening a can of worms.

Communication was made difficult for the fact that the international studio was extremely busy, and even being put through to his contact person was a tough nut to crack.

On top of that, the meetings were constantly being put back or put forward, producing a destabilizing effect on his own studio's workflow.

He put all of this down to the huge dimensions of this project, and he had always been ready to go the extra mile to do things well. Now, though, after eight months like this, he was starting to doubt how long he would still be able to put up with this stressful situation.

He felt he needed a break, however short, to catch his breath. His best friend Jack might be what he needed. He was a successful writer, and he lived on a small island on the Hudson River. Peter called him up and asked him if he could put him up for a night. Jack was engaged in the final stages of his latest book, but he immediately said yes to his friend.

Jack was the perfect friend for Peter. He was always ready to lend a sympathetic ear, and never put him

Text 2 🎧 24

Peter had felt thrilled when his architecture studio had won the bid to build one of the most prestigious skyscrapers in Manhattan in collaboration with the best international architecture studio of all time. He felt this was a very special opportunity. In fact, it was. What he had not realized was that this was going to be all except easy. Every time a problem arose, it led to a lot more other problems.

Communication was made difficult for the fact that the international studio was extremely busy, and even managing to be connected on the phone to his contact person was really tough.

On top of that, the meetings were constantly being postponed or moved to an earlier time or date, producing a destabilizing effect on his own studio's workflow.

He attributed the cause of all this to the huge dimensions of this project, and had always been ready to exceed expectations to do things well. Now, though, after eight months like this, he was starting to doubt how long he would still be able to tolerate this stressful situation.

He felt he needed a break, however short, to rest a bit. His best friend Jack might be what he needed. He was a successful writer, and he lived on a small island on the Hudson River. Peter called him and asked him if he could host him for a night. Jack was engaged in the final stages of his latest book, but he immediately said yes to his friend.

Jack was the perfect friend for Peter. He was always ready to listen to him with sympathy, and never down or put him off. He spoke little, but he was always supportive.

The two friends met. Peter put on some comfortable clothes. Jack had put on the lights for dinner, but after dinner he put them out and the two friends sat out on the patio by the fire pit. They talked till late, until the fire burnt itself out. At last, Jack put out his cigar, and they went to bed.

The next day, Peter felt full of energy and optimistic again. After all, the end of the project was in sight. He just had to grin and bear it for a little longer.

In the end, Peter's patience, competence, and endurance paid off his efforts. His studio gained its well-deserved visibility and became one of the most sought after in the field.

Sometimes, a bumpy ride might indeed turn out to be a blessing in disguise.

belittle him or demoralize him. He spoke little, but he was always supportive.

The two friends met. Peter wore some comfortable clothes. Jack had turned on the lights for dinner, but after dinner he turned them off and the two friends sat out on the patio by the fire pit. They talked till late, until the fire ceased to burn. At last, Jack extinguished his cigar, and then they went to bed.

The next day, Peter felt full of energy and optimistic again. After all, the end of the project was near. He just had to resist a little longer.

In the end, Peter's patience, competence and endurance met his efforts with success. His studio gained its well-deserved visibility and became one of the most desired in the field.

Sometimes, a hard time might indeed reveal itself to be a very good thing.

Vocabulary

Be on top of the world (idiom) = _____

Put (sth) up (phrasal verb) = _____

A once-in-a-lifetime opportunity (collocation) =

_____

All but = _____

Smooth sailing (idiom) = _____

Open a can of worms (idiom) = _____

Put (sb) through to (sb) (phrasal verb) =

_____

A tough nut to crack (idiom) = _____

Put (sth) back/ off (or push sth back) (phrasal verb) =

_____

CHAPTER 12: PUT — A BUMPY RIDE

Put (sth) forward (or Bring sth forward) (phrasal verb) =

_____

Put (sth) down to (phrasal verb) =   _____

Go the extra mile (idiom) =   _____

Put up with (sth) (phrasal verb) =   _____

Catch one's breath (idiom) =   _____

Call (sb) up (phrasal verb) =   _____

Put (sb) up (phrasal verb) =   _____

Lend a sympathetic ear (idiom) =   _____

Put (sb) down (phrasal verb) =   _____

Put (sb) off (phrasal verb) =   _____

Put (sth) on (1) (phrasal verb) =   _____

Put (sth) on (2) (phrasal verb) =   _____

Put (sth) out (1) (phrasal verb) =   _____

Burn (sth) out (phrasal verb) =   _____

Put (sth) out (2) (phrasal verb) =   _____

The end is in sight (phrase) =   _____

Grin and bear it (idiom) =   _____

Pay off the effort (idiom) =   _____

Pay (sth) off (phrasal verb) =   to pay a debt/mortgage etc. in full

A bumpy ride (idiom) =   _____

Turn out (phrasal verb) =   _____

A blessing in disguise (idiom) =   _____

Exercise 12.1 🎧 23

Listen to text n. 1 while following along from text 2.

Exercise 12.2 🎧 24

Listen to text n. 2 while following along from text 1.

Exercise 12.3

Read the two texts, and complete the phrasal verbs and idiomatic expressions with their meaning.

Exercise 12.4

Listen to text n. 1 again, press pause after each sentence, and repeat.

Exercise 12.5

Put the correct preposition or particle next to the verb "PUT", choosing among: DOWN, DOWN TO, BACK, FORWARD, OFF, ON (x2), OUT (x2), UP, UP WITH, THROUGH TO.

PUT DOWN	PUT FORWARD	PUT OUT (X2)	PUT UP WITH
PUT DOWN TO	PUT OFF	PUT UP	PUT THROUGH TO
PUT BACK/OFF	PUT ON (X2)		

1) The meeting has been _____ (moved to an earlier time) an hour. So, it's not at 4:00 pm but at 3:00 pm.

2) The teacher _____ the students' bad behavior _____ (attributed the cause) his own inexperience with class management.

3) The firefighters were able to _____ (extinguish) the fire after an hour.

4) Please, when you _____ (turn on) the lights, remember to _____ them _____ (turn off).

5) The Berlin Wall was _____ (built, erected) in 1961, and it was broken down in 1989.

6) As she was cold, she _____ (wore) a jacket.

7) Parents should not _____ their children _____ (criticize, belittle). They should praise them when they do something good.

8) (On the phone) Hello, I'm calling to ask if it would be possible to _____ (postpone) our appointment of Friday at 10:00 am, as another commitment came up.

9) (On the phone) One moment, I will _____ you _____ (connect with) customer care.

10) Carla really wanted to take up martial arts, but she was _____ (demoralized) by the sight of all those people throwing each other on the floor.

11) When Paul and Mary had their first baby, they had to _____ (tolerate) many sleepless nights.

12) We will spend New Year's Eve in Venice. A friend of ours will _____ us _____ (host) for the night.

Exercise 12.6

Put the correct preposition or particle next to the verb "PUT", choosing among:
DOWN, DOWN TO, BACK, FORWARD, OFF, ON (x2), OUT (x2), UP, UP WITH, THROUGH TO.

1) Laura wasn't willing to put _____ her friend's continuous lies, and broke up their friendship.

2) Could you put me _____ the sales manager, please?

3) Please, put _____ your cigarette before coming in. This is a no-smoking area.

4) Tom's manager would always put him _____ for the slightest mistakes.

5) Mike's father would often try and put him _____ from his dream of becoming a guitar player. He thought a job in a bank was a safer choice.

6) Since it was extremely sunny, she put _____ a hat before going out.

7) Who put _____ the light again? I thought I had put it _____ .

8) Have you heard? They are going to put _____ a new shopping mall in that area.

9) Can global warming be put _____ an increase in pollution, or do you think there are other causes as well?

10) We decided to put _____ the conference call to next week.

11) I prefer to put my commitments _____ whenever possible. The earlier, the better.

12) When I went to London, looking for a job and accommodation, a friend of mine put me _____ until I found a room in a host family.

Exercise 12.7

Complete the sentences with the following phrasal verbs:

Call up, Pay off, Turn off, Turn on, Turn out, Burn out

1) My brother and his wife have _____ (paid in full) their mortgage and now they are free.

2) Please, _____ (stop the noise) the radio. I'm studying.

3) My sister _____ me _____ (phoned) and told me the good news.

4) Since it was getting dark out, he _____ (activated) the light in the room.

5) Unfortunately, buying that car _____ (revealed itself) to be a bad decision as we always use the subway to go to work.

6) If no one rekindles the fire, it will _____ (cease to have flames).

Exercise 12.8

Complete the text with the following phrasal verbs: *Call up, Pay off, Turn off, Turn on, Turn out*

As Paul 1) _____ his loan for the solar panels, he immediately 2) _____ his friend to tell him the good news and celebrate together. The solar panels 3) _____ to be a great decision because he found a way to apply the stored energy to his electricity grid as well. He was still careful to 4) _____ the lights whenever he didn't need them, but now he found a certain satisfaction when he 5) _____ them _____ knowing that he was using sustainable energy.

Exercise 12.9

Complete the sentences using: Phrasal Verbs with PUT + DOWN, DOWN TO, BACK, FORWARD, OFF (x2), ON (x2), OUT (x2), UP, UP WITH, THROUGH TO and

Call up, Pay off, Turn off, Turn on, Turn out, Bring forward

1) _____ and _____ are synonyms when you want to have the light or an electric device on.

2) _____ and _____ are synonyms when you want to have light or an electric device off.

CHAPTER 12: PUT — A BUMPY RIDE

3) Many people tried to _____ her _____ from her dream of _____ ing _____ an apartment on the top floor of the house, but in the end she worked hard and _____ her debts. Now she lives on the top floor, and she rents the bottom floor.

4) What's a synonym of "postpone"? "_____."

5) What are the two phrasal verbs to use when you want to arrange a meeting at an earlier time? _____ or _____.

6) Unfortunately, Lauren had a particular colleague who would always _____ her _____ for using different procedures to carry out their job. She _____ her behavior _____ the fact that this person was not very happy with her life, in general. That is why, most of the time, she was able to _____ such gratuitous criticism. It _____ to be a good choice because she was promoted, and her colleague wasn't.

7) If you want to _____ a candle properly, you shouldn't blow it out, but you should use a candle snuffer.

8) (On the phone) A: May I speak to your boss, please?
B: Yes, certainly. I will _____ you _____ him immediately, sir.

9) Jane's mother _____ her _____ to ask what she wanted for dinner, but Jane was busy and had to call her back.

10) Would you please _____ me _____ for a couple of nights while I'm in your town for business? Thank you so much!

Exercise 12.10

Look at Text 1 and write these sentences using an idiom, a phrase, or a collocation:

BE ON TOP OF THE WORLD

SMOOTH SAILING

A ONCE-IN-A-LIFETIME OPPORTUNITY

OPEN A CAN OF WORMS

A TOUGH NUT TO CRACK

GO THE EXTRA MILE

CATCH ONE'S BREATH

LEND A SYMPATHETIC EAR

THE END IS IN SIGHT

PAY OFF THE EFFORT

A BUMPY RIDE

A BLESSING IN DISGUISE

GRIN AND BEAR IT

CHAPTER 12: PUT — A BUMPY RIDE

1) I ran too fast. I need to stop and <u>rest</u>.

_____

2) When the plumber tried to fix the leakage in the shower, he found that <u>there were a lot more prob-lems to solve.</u>

_____

_____

3) That person is really <u>difficult to deal with</u>!

_____

4) The project was <u>tough</u> from the beginning, but it turned out to be <u>a good thing</u> because it opened up lots of other job opportunities.

_____

_____

5) The hike should be <u>easy</u>. It says here that it's for families with children.

_____

_____

6) Lauren always <u>exceeds expectations</u> in doing her job. She should get a promotion.

_____

_____

7) Paul is an excellent friend. He's always ready <u>to listen to your problems.</u>

_____

_____

8) As <u>the end was visible</u>, the runner sped up and won the race. He was <u>exhilarated</u>. All his training had <u>brought him success</u>.

_____

_____

9) Of course you should accept the offer. It's <u>a unique opportunity that will never present itself again</u>!

_____

_____

10) The race is almost over! He just has to <u>resist</u> a little longer, and then he will have finished!

_____

_____

CHAPTER 13: RUN/SET — THE SALT OF THE EARTH

Text 1 🎧 25

Some people are naturally talented... in everything. This was the case for Anthony. An only child, born of parents already on in years, Anthony was always well-groomed, well-behaved, and well-organized.

What set him apart from the rest of us was his sharpness, his beautifully logical mind, along with a keen sense of ambition.

He didn't need to run after the best results. He got them apparently without sweating it, unlike me, for example. He just ran over the lesson once, and it was learned. There's to say that whenever he set about dealing with a challenging task, nothing would set him back.

Did I mention how vivid his imagination was? He never ran out of original ideas. Working in a team with him was just a pleasure. How about his mental organization? Whenever we worked in groups, he would set out a detailed report, which was the ace up his sleeve to get us good grades.

He was also very down to earth and inclusive: he always ran his ideas by his team members and listened to everyone's input. He was the apple of the teacher's eye!

He was well loved by most of his classmates. Some of them, however, green with envy, would have loved to see him run over by a bicycle. They would have happily set their hamster* on him, or at least see him run into something difficult, for once.

Text 2 🎧 26

Some people are naturally talented... in everything. This was the case for Anthony. An only child, born of not so young parents, Anthony was always well-groomed, well-behaved, and well-organized.

What made him different from the rest of us was his sharpness, his beautifully logical mind, along with a keen sense of ambition.

He did not need to persistently pursue the best results. He got them apparently without worrying about it, unlike me, for example. He just quickly read the lesson once, and it was learned. There is to say that whenever he started dealing with a challenging task, nothing would delay him.

Did I mention how imaginative he was? He never finished his supply of original ideas. Working in a team with him was just a pleasure. How about his mental organization? Whenever we worked in groups, he would write down a clear and detailed report, which was his secret resource to get us good grades.

He was also very practical, unpretentious and inclusive: he always told his ideas to his team members to get their opinion and listened to everyone's input. He was the teachers' favorite!

He was well loved by most of his classmates. Some of them, however, envious of him, would have loved to see him hit by a bicycle, have their hamster attack him, or at least see him experience something difficult, for once.

I never despised him, though. Rather, I admired him. How could I not? He was <u>a good egg</u>, as well as <u>a smart cookie</u>.

Well, at any rate, I <u>ran into</u> him the other day. He was here in town on a brief vacation with his wife and two children. After graduating from Harvard, he <u>set out</u> on a journey to the Middle East. There he met his wife, a British doctor. He said that after a bomb was <u>set off</u> in a school one night, as a warning against education, he felt compelled to do something. He <u>set up</u> another school, where he personally teaches every day, with courage and determination. He is, indeed, <u>the salt of the earth</u>.

I never disliked him, though. Rather, I admired him. How could I not? He was <u>a good person</u>, as well as <u>intelligent</u>.

Well, at any rate, I <u>met him by chance</u> the other day. He was here in town on a brief vacation with his wife and two children. After graduating from Harvard, he <u>left</u> on a journey to the Middle East. There he met his wife, a British doctor. He said that after a bomb <u>exploded</u> in a school one night, as a warning against education, he felt compelled to do something. He <u>established</u> another school, where he personally teaches every day, with courage and determination. He is, indeed, <u>a fine and noble person who deserves respect for what he does</u>.

Note: "Set a hamster on someone" is not a common expression. The author did not want to incite violence.

Vocabulary:

Be on in years (idiom) = _____

Set (sb) apart from (phrasal verb) = _____

Run after (sth/ sb) (phrasal verb) = _____

Not sweat sth (phrase) = _____

Run over (sth) (phrasal verb) = _____

Set about (sth) (phrasal verb) = _____

Set (sb/sth) back (phrasal verb) = _____

Have a vivid imagination (collocation) = _____

Run out of (sth) (phrasal verb) = _____

Set (sth) out (phrasal verb) = _____

Have an ace up one's sleeve (idiom) = _____

Be down to earth (idiom) = _____

Run (sth) by (sb) = _____

Be the apple of one's eye (idiom) = _____

Be green with envy (idiom) = _____

Run (sb/sth) over (phrasal verb) = _____

Set (sb/sth) on (sb) (phrasal verb) = _____

Run into (sth) (phrasal verb) = _____

Be a good egg (idiom) = _____

Be a smart cookie (idiom) = _____

Run into (sb) (phrasal verb) = _____

Set out/off (phrasal verb) = _____

Set (sth) off (phrasal verb)= _____

Set (sth) up (phrasal verb) = _____

Be the salt of the earth (idiom) = _____

Exercise 13.1 🎧 25

Listen to text n. 1 while following along from text 2.

Exercise 13.2 🎧 26

Listen to text n. 2 while following along from text 1.

Exercise 13.3

Read the two texts, and complete the phrasal verbs and idiomatic expressions with their meaning.

Exercise 13.4

Listen to text n. 1 again, press pause after each sentence, and repeat.

Exercise 13.5

Put the correct preposition or particle next to the verb "RUN", choosing among: INTO (x2), AFTER, OUT OF, OVER (x2), BY.

RUN INTO (X2)	RUN OUT OF	RUN BY
RUN AFTER	RUN OVER (X2)	

1) We _____ (finished) milk. We need to buy more.

2) Slow down, please. You almost _____ (hit) that tire in the middle of the road.

3) When Kate moved back to London after many years, she _____ (met by chance) her first love. They fell in love again, and they got married.

4) We _____ (found) some problems with the development of the software, which I would like to _____ (talk to for solutions) my boss.

5) All his life he _____ (persistently pursued) glory and fame.

6) He _____ (quickly read) his notes one last time before the presentation.

Exercise 13.6

Put the correct preposition or particle next to the verb "RUN", choosing among: INTO (x2), AFTER, OUT OF, OVER (x2), BY.

1) Your sister ran _____ Jason yesterday. He sends his regards.

2) Your dog is constantly running _____ cats. Yesterday it was almost run _____ by a car. You should do something about it. You may run _____ legal problems.

3) Before making a decision about this job offer, he ran it _____ his girlfriend.

4) We ran _____ coffee in my office, and the next shipment isn't arriving until next week.

5) Let's run _____ the main points again before going over to the next chapter.

Exercise 13.7

Put the correct preposition or particle next to the verb "SET", choosing among: ABOUT, APART, BACK, OUT/OFF, OFF (X2), ON, UP, OUT.

SET ABOUT	SET OUT/OFF	SET UP
SET APART	SET OFF (X2)	SET OUT
SET BACK	SET ON	

1) He wants to _____ (leave) early to avoid the hottest hours of the day.

2) "Romeo, If you don't leave Juliet alone, I'll _____ her cousins _____ you (cause them to attack you)," said Mr. Capuleti. (From the play *Romeo and Juliet*, by William Shakespeare)

3) He _____ (started dealing with) the difficult task, but then he was _____ (delayed) by a phone call. He should have turned off his phone.

4) What _____ her _____ (differentiated) from her classmates at the school for hairdressers is that she _____ (established) her own hair salon, whereas the others didn't.

5) A seagull landed on my car and _____ (triggered) my car alarm.

6) The incident _____ (triggered) a lot of protests and riots, which then culminated in the French Revolution.

7) The contract was _____ (written clearly) point by point.

Exercise 13.8

Put the correct preposition or particle next to the verb "SET", choosing among: ABOUT, APART, BACK, OUT/OFF, OFF, ON, UP, OUT.

1) The approval of the reforms were set _____ by the continuous disagreements between the parties.

2) They set _____ yesterday on their trip to Norway.

3) Their product set itself _____ from the rest because of its great quality and captivating design.

4) The police set their dogs _____ the criminals.

5) We should set _____ the assignment. It's not easy, and the sooner we start the better.

6) Jack set _____ his company forty years ago.

7) The terrorists set _____ a bomb in the newspaper headquarters, but fortunately nobody got injured.

8) Being very organized, she set _____ a very clear outline of the lesson.

Exercise 13.9

Complete the sentences using: Phrasal Verbs with RUN + INTO (x2), AFTER, OUT OF, OVER (x2), BY and

SET + ABOUT, APART, BACK, OUT/OFF, OFF, ON, UP, OUT.

1) We were to _____ to go to the beach, but we _____ a major drainage problem in the toilet, which _____ us _____ .

2) The police _____ the thief, but it wasn't until they _____ their dogs _____ him that they were able to catch him.

3) Let's go single file while walking on the side of the street. We don't want to be _____ by a car.

4) The dancers _____ their dance routine once more, before the show.

5) The provocation _____ an uproar of public indignation.

6) Whenever he _____ energy, he retired to his secret spot up the hills and sat for an hour in nature.

7) The committee _____ (started) in _____ ing _____ the rules to follow.

8) I have a couple of doubts. Can I _____ them _____ you?

9) Andrew _____ an old classmate. He has _____ his own business. Although it is still quite small, what _____ him _____ from his competitors is that he is very kind and polite.

Exercise 13.10

Look at Text 1 and write these sentences using an idiom, a phrase, or a collocation:

BE/ GET ON IN YEARS	BE THE APPLE OF ONE'S EYE
DON'T SWEAT IT	BE GREEN WITH ENVY
HAVE A VIVID IMAGINATION	BE A GOOD EGG
(HAVE AN) ACE UP ONE'S SLEEVE	BE A SMART COOKIE
BE DOWN TO EARTH	BE THE SALT OF THE EARTH

1) Mother Theresa from Calcutta was a very special individual.

   _____

2) John is such a good person! He would never envy you.

   _____

3) He has a great imagination. That's his secret to overcome difficult situations.

   _____

4) Jessica is very clever. She always makes smart decisions.

   _____

5) People who have met this actor say that he is very simple, practical and unpretentious.

   _____

6) Don't worry! I'm sure you'll be ok tomorrow!

   _____

7) Despite the fact that Mark and his wife are getting old, they still look great.

   _____

CHAPTER 14: TAKE — TWO PEAS IN A POD

Text 1 🎧 27

"Indeed, your sister and you are like two peas in a pod!".

 That is what grandma used to tell me about my twin sister Lauren and I, and how we had also amazingly taken after our mother. The way I tilted my head when I was puzzled about something, the way I was always ready to take something back if I realized I was at fault... these and other features of both my appearance and personality used to take grandma back in time.

Grandma would often take a walk down memory lane, to a time when both mom and aunt Sara were little. As they grew up, aunt Sara moved to Australia, and mom and dad got married. Then, tragically, both our parents passed away when we were very young, and Lauren was taken in by aunt Sara in Australia, whereas I was taken in by grandma in Italy.

I know it sounds like the plot of a film, "identical twins separated at an early age"... and although it may seem cruel, at the time, it seemed like the best thing to do. In fact, we turned out fine, I'd say. We were constantly in touch both over the phone and by mail. Yes, because when we were growing up the internet was yet to be invented. But it didn't matter: we never grew apart. They say "blood is thicker than water". For us, it was so.

It was amazing how, unbeknownst to each other, we would take up the same hobby at the same time. Sometimes we would even try something on, buy it but take it back to the store on the same day!

Text 2 🎧 28

"Indeed, your sister and you are extremely similar to each other!"

That is what grandma used to tell me about my twin sister Lauren and I, and how, we also amazingly resembled our mother. The way I moved my head on one side when I was confused about something, the way I was always ready to admit I was wrong if I realized I had made a mistake...these and other features of both my appearance and personality used to make grandma remember about the past.

Memories would often come to grandma's mind, back when both mom and aunt Sara were little. As they became older, aunt Sara moved to Australia, and mom and dad got married. Then, tragically, both our parents died when we were very young, and Lauren was taken to live with aunt Sara in Australia, whereas I was taken to live with grandma in Italy.

I know it sounds like the plot of a film, "identical twins separated when they were very young"... and although it may seem cruel, at the time, it seemed like the best thing to do. In fact, the result was good, I would say. We were constantly communicating both over the phone and by mail. Yes, because when we were growing up the internet was yet to be invented. But it did not matter: we never stopped being friends. They say "family bonds are extremely strong." For us, it was so.

It was amazing how, without the other one knowing it, we would become interested in the same hobby at the same time. Sometimes we would even put on some clothes to see if they fit, buy them but return them to the store on the same day!

It wasn't until we both graduated from high school that we were able to physically see each other. I was taken on by a beauty salon, and as soon as I made enough money to get a plane ticket, I took a month off work and I set off to Melbourne. I still remember feeling butterflies in my stomach when the plane was taking off.

When we met, it was indeed as if we had never been apart. Would you imagine that when we took off our clothes and put on our pajamas, we found out that we even had some beauty marks in the same spots?

Anyways, when aunt Sara and Lauren took me out to restaurants, movie theaters, etc. I was amazed at the laid-back atmosphere of the city, but it still wasn't enough to make me want to move there, yet.

As heartbreaking as living far away from my sister was, I carried on with my life in Italy. Grandma wasn't growing any younger, and she was the only immediate family I had.

At work, things were taking off. My boss had proposed that I run a branch of her beauty salon and I happily took on her offer.

Life was good. Or good enough. My sister was still on the other side of the world and I missed her greatly. I gradually started to take to the idea of living there.

It only came natural to take the leap of faith after grandma passed away. Years have gone by now. I run my own beauty salon in Melbourne. Both my sister and I are married and bought a duplex. Our daughters are growing up like sisters, and indeed they bear such a striking resemblance that when they are seen together, people say "They are just like two peas in a pod!"

It was not until we both graduated from high school that we were able to physically see each other. I was hired by a beauty salon, and as soon as I made enough money to get a plane ticket, I had a month long vacation and left for Melbourne. I still remember feeling really nervous and excited when the plane was leaving the ground.

When we met, it was indeed as if we had never been apart. Would you imagine that when we removed our clothes and wore our pajamas, we discovered that we even had some beauty marks in the same spots?

Anyways, when aunt Sara and Lauren invited me to restaurants, movie theaters, etc. I was amazed at the relaxed atmosphere of the city, but it still wasn't enough to make me want to move there, yet.

As sad as living far away from my sister was, I continued my life in Italy. Grandma was getting old, and she was the only close family I had.

At work, things were rapidly and unexpectedly improving. My boss had proposed that I manage a branch of her beauty salon and I happily accepted her offer.

Life was good. Or good enough. My sister was still on the other side of the world and I missed her greatly. I gradually started to like the idea of living there.

It only came natural to make the decision despite its uncertainties after grandma died. Years have passed now. I have my own beauty salon in Melbourne. Both my sister and I are married and bought a duplex. Our daughters are growing up like sisters, and indeed they look so similar that when they are seen together, people say "They look incredibly alike!"

Vocabulary:

Be like two peas in a pod (Idiom) = _____

Take after (sb) (phrasal verb) = _____

Take (sth) back (1) (phrasal verb) = _____

Be at fault (phrase) = _____

Take (sb) back (to the past) (phrasal verb) =

_____

Take a walk/trip down memory lane (idiom) =

_____

Grow up (phrasal verb) = _____

Pass away (phrasal verb) = _____

Take (sb) in (phrasal verb) = _____

At an early age (phrase) = _____

Turn out (phrasal verb) = _____

Be in touch (phrase) = _____

Grow apart (phrasal verb) = _____

Blood is thicker than water (proverb) =

_____

Unbeknownst to sb (phrase) = _____

Take up (sth) (phrasal verb) = _____

Try (sth) on (phrasal verb) = _____

Take (sth) back (2) (phrasal verb) = _____

Take (sb) on (phrasal verb) = _____

Take (time/days..) off (phrasal verb) =

_____

Set off/out (phrasal verb) = _____

Have butterflies in one's stomach (idiom) =

_____

Take off (plane) (1) (phrasal verb) = _____

Take (sth) off (phrasal verb) = _____

Find (sth) out (phrasal verb) = _____

Take (sb) out (phrasal verb) = _____

Laid-back (adjective) = _____

Heartbreaking (adjective) = _____

Carry on (phrasal verb) = _____

Not be growing any younger (phrase) =

_____

Immediate family (collocation) = _____

Take off (2) (phrasal verb) = _____

Run a business/ a branch/ a store (collocation) =

_____

Take (sth) on (phrasal verb) = _____

Take to (sb/sth) (phrasal verb) = _____

Take a leap of faith (idiom) = _____

Bear a striking resemblance to sb (phrase) =

_____

Exercise 14 🎧 27

Listen to text n. 1 while following along from text 2.

Exercise 14.2 🎧 28

Listen to text n. 2 while following along from text 1.

Exercise 14.3

Read the two texts, and complete the phrasal verbs and idiomatic expressions with their meaning.

Exercise 14.4

Listen to text n. 1 again, press pause after each sentence, and repeat.

Exercise 14.5

Put the correct preposition or particle next to the verb "TAKE", choosing among: AFTER, BACK (x2), IN, OFF (x3), ON (x2), OUT, UP, TO.

TAKE AFTER	TAKE IN	TAKE ON (x2)	TAKE UP
TAKE BACK (x2)	TAKE OFF (x3)	TAKE OUT	TAKE TO

1) The plane _____ (left the ground) this morning at 8:00 am.

2) In my opinion, he _____ (accepts) too many projects at the same time.

3) My sister _____ (looks similar to) my father, while I look more like my mother.

4) She had been acting as a minor character in many movies, but her career really _____ (dramatically improved) with an extremely successful TV series.

5) If she got offended, you should just _____ (admit you made a mistake) what you said.

6) Once at home, Maria noticed that the shirt was faulty, and _____ it _____ (returned) to the store.

7) If you are hot, _____ (remove) your coat while we are still inside.

8) When I studied at college, I had to move to another city. My aunt, who lived there, _____ me _____ (let me stay at her house) until I found my own accommodation.

9) Paul and John _____ (started) fishing when they were very young.

10) My company _____ (hired) a new secretary. She's still learning.

11) He _____ her _____ (invited her to a restaurant) for dinner on their third date.

12) This song _____ me _____ (makes me remember) to my teenage years.

13) He _____ (started to like) soccer right away. Now he goes to soccer practice thrice a week.

Exercise 14.6

Put the correct preposition or particle next to the verb "TAKE", choosing among:
AFTER, BACK (x2), IN, OFF (x3), ON (x2), OUT, UP.

1) The plane hasn't taken _____ yet due to a traffic jam on the runway.

2) I think Mike takes _____ his grandfather, rather than his parents.

3) When Peter was taken _____ by the BBC as a sound engineer, he saw that his career was finally taking _____. He took his girlfriend _____ for dinner to celebrate.

4) Would you ever take _____ some exchange students in your house?

5) I think I will take this sweater _____ . It's too big.

6) Anne is really talented. She should take _____ painting.

7) My cat and my dog didn't take _____ each other right away, but now they get on well.

8) A: I think we still have one more pair of jeans in that size. Oops, sorry. I take that _____. This pair is the last one.

9) B: Ok, I'll buy them. But I won't take them _____. I'm going to keep them on.

10) Roger took _____ the position of head teacher at the language school.

11) My grandma loves showing me old pictures. It takes her _____ to when she was younger.

Exercise 14.7

Complete the sentences with the following phrasal verbs:

Grow up, Pass away, Turn out, Grow apart, Try on, Set off/out, Find out, Carry on.

1) When Jason _____ (discovered) that his cousin had _____ (died), they had _____ (stopped being close friends) for a long time. He was sorry about it.

2) When Peter _____ (became an adult), he became a doctor as he had always dreamt of.

3) After the concert, Mark found it difficult to _____ (continue) with his daily life for a while. He couldn't take his mind off it.

4) The researchers weren't sure about their course of action, but the experiment results _____ (revealed themselves) as expected.

5) Karin hates shopping for clothes online. She prefers to _____ them _____ (wear for a moment) at a physical store.

6) He _____ (left) earlier this morning because he had a meeting at work.

Exercise 14.8

Complete the text with the following phrasal verbs:

Grow up, Pass away, Turn out, Grow apart, Try on, Set off/out, Find out, Carry on.

Jack and Susanne 1) _____ together and fell in love during high school. As they each went to different colleges, they gradually 2) _____ and broke up. Each of them 3) _____ with their lives and forgot about each other. After ten years, unfortunately, a class-mate of theirs 4) _____ unexpectedly. They immediately 5) _____ to their home town to participate in the class reunion. Susanne needed to buy some clothes for the occasion, so she went into the local store. As she was 6) _____ ing _____ some pants, she heard his voice. As it 7) _____, he also needed to buy clothes. After spending some time together, they 8) _____ that they were still in love with each other, and they didn't even remember why they had broken up. They got married the following year.

Exercise 14.9

Complete the sentences using: Phrasal Verbs with TAKE + AFTER, BACK (x2), IN, OFF (x3), ON (x2), OUT, UP, TO and *Grow up, Pass away, Turn out, Grow apart, Try on, Set off/out, Find out, Carry on.*

1) No-one in the family was sure who Mary had _____ since she didn't really bear any strik-ing resemblance to anyone in her immediate family. It _____ that she looked exactly like a great-aunt on her mother's side.

2) Hmm... I don't quite like red on you. How about you _____ the red shirt _____ and _____ the dark blue one _____ ?

3) They _____ extra early to get to the airport on time. Unfortunately, once they arrived, they _____ that the airplane wouldn't _____ that day, due to severe turbulence.

4) Please, _____ talking. I'm sorry I interrupted you.

5) Paul and Mark were best friends when they were children, but as it often happens, they _____ when they _____.

6) I'm sorry. It was a mean thing to say. I _____ it _____. Please, accept my apologies.

7) I'm sorry to hear that his dog _____. I know how much he loved him.

8) He _____ tennis as soon as he _____ it _____.

9) Her career as a scientist really _____ when she was _____ by an American college.

10) Working mothers _____ a lot of responsibilities.

11) The setting _____ the spectator _____ to the fifties very convincingly.

12) As the kitten didn't have anywhere else to go, the elderly lady _____ it _____ with her, and now they are inseparable companions.

13) When your cousin came for a visit, did you _____ her _____ to a local food festival?

Exercise 14.10

Look at Text 1 and write these sentences using an idiom, a phrase, or a collocation:

BE LIKE TWO PEAS IN A POD	HAVE BUTTERFLIES IN ONE'S STOMACH
BE AT FAULT	NOT BE GROWING ANY YOUNGER
TAKE A WALK/TRIP DOWN MEMORY LANE	IMMEDIATE FAMILY
AT AN EARLY AGE	RUN A BUSINESS/COMPANY
BE/KEEP IN TOUCH	TAKE A LEAP OF FAITH
BLOOD IS THICKER THAN WATER	BEAR A STRIKING RESEMBLANCE TO (sb)
UNBEKNOWNST TO (sb)	

1) The two brothers resemble each other a lot. They look extremely similar.

_____

_____

2) Without her knowing it, he had already ordered pizza. So, when she arrived, dinner was ready.

_____

_____

3) Choosing a career path when you are very young is like making a decision despite all its uncertainties.

_____

_____

4) Jack has been managing his own company for over 40 years.

_____

5) The two friends have kept communicating with each other since they were young.

_____

_____

6) Even if someone in your close family made a mistake, you should always forgive them. Family bonds will always be stronger than anything else.

_____

_____

7) Since the two friends were getting older, they would often recollect their past memories together.

_____

_____

8) Every time, before sitting an exam, he had a nervous feeling in his stomach.

_____

CHAPTER 15: TURN — A DOG'S LIFE

Text 1 🎧 29

Nerino turned around. With a heavy heart and an empty stomach, he stared at the kitchen of that tempting restaurant. He could only imagine what sort of treats and delights were hiding in that paradise. That is, because he was punctually turned away by the kitchen staff. He was starving and desperate for food. How he had ended up in that situation, he couldn't tell, and perhaps at this point, it was water under the bridge. Who could he turn to? How to sort this out? He just did what he knew best: roaming and hunting.

Although so far he had managed to still be in one piece, life as a stray cat was far from pleasant. Especially when it rained or when it got cold. Ironically, he was truly leading a "dog's life".

One night, he came across a wonderful yard. In the middle of it was a beautiful house. Everything was pitch dark around him, except for the warm light coming from the kitchen in the back. There was a French window* that offered a full view of the occupants inside. A family of three was having dinner. How he longed to have a scrap of their food. At that moment, he felt two eyes fixing inquisitively on him. Then he heard a voice from the mother "There are two green eyes out there... And they're staring at me...".

That's all Julie could see that night because the lights outside were off and Nerino was black. She opened the door and turned on the light. Nerino ran a little farther away, at a safe distance, as he was a scaredy cat.

Text 2 🎧 30

Nerino looked back. With a sad heart and an empty stomach, he stared at the kitchen of that tempting restaurant. He could only imagine what sort of treats and delights were hiding in that paradise. That is, because he was punctually refused admittance by the kitchen staff. He was starving and desperate for food. How he had ultimately found himself in that situation, he couldn't tell, and perhaps at this point, it was not a matter of importance any more.

Who could he ask for help and assistance? How could he solve this problem? He just did what he knew best: roaming and hunting. Although so far he had managed to be unharmed, life as a stray cat was far from pleasant. Especially when it rained or it got cold. He was truly leading an unhappy existence full of difficulties.

One night, he found himself in a wonderful yard, by chance. In the middle of it was a beautiful house. Everything was completely dark around him, except for the warm light coming from the kitchen in the back. There was a French window that offered a full view of the occupants inside. A family of three was having dinner. How he longed to have a piece of their food. At that moment, he felt two eyes fixing inquisitively on him. Then he heard a voice from the mother "There are two green eyes out there... And they are staring at me...".

That is all Julie could see that night because the lights outside were off and Nerino was black. She opened the door and switched on the light. Nerino ran a little farther away, at a safe distance, as he was a timid creature, easily scared by everything.

Julie took some ham from the fridge, cut it up and put it in a bowl, and in another one she poured in some water. Then she closed the door and turned off the light. Although Nerino knew all the family was looking at him through the French window, he ate with profound delight.

Over the next few days, whenever Nerino turned up, his implicit request was never turned down. Every time, he could find something delicious that never turned him off, as he had heard of other cats. As he called in on them more often, he noticed that the food became more and more elaborate: tuna, salmon, beef. Not only that, but in time, a nice cushion appeared on the veranda, perfect for a nice nap in the morning sun. And the family was just adorable. Father, mother, and little daughter were always ready to pet him and welcome him in.

Well, as you have probably figured out, it turned out that Nerino found a home here where he was loved and pampered. From the scrawny little cat he was, he turned into a majestic handsome black cat, with shiny fur and long whiskers, and never had to beg for food again. He lived a long and happy life with his masters, who, in turn, found an affectionate and intelligent companion

Julie took some ham from the fridge, cut it in little pieces and put it in a bowl, and in another one she put some water. Then she closed the door and switched off the light. Although Nerino knew all the family was looking at him through the French window, he ate with profound delight.

Over the next few days, whenever Nerino arrived unexpectedly, his implicit request was never refused. Every time, he could find something delicious that never made him lose interest, as he had heard of other cats. As he paid them a short visit more often, he noticed that the food became more and more elaborate: tuna, salmon, beef. Not only that, but in time, a nice cushion appeared on the veranda, perfect for a nice nap in the morning sun. And the family was just adorable. Father, mother, and little daughter were always ready to pet him and welcome him in.

Well, as you have probably understood, it happened that Nerino found a home here where he was loved and pampered. From the thin and weak little cat he was, he became a majestic handsome black cat, with shiny fur and long whiskers, and never had to beg for food again. He lived a long and happy life with his masters, who, in turn, found an affectionate and intelligent companion.

Note: A French window is a door made entirely of glass.

Vocabulary:

Turn around (phrasal verb) =	turn yourself in the opposite direction
With a heavy heart (collocation) =	_____
Turn (sb) away (phrasal verb) =	_____
End up (phrasal verb) =	_____
It's water under the bridge (idiom) =	_____

Turn to (phrasal verb) = _____

Sort (sth) out (phrasal verb) = _____

In one piece (idiom) = _____

A dog's life (idiom) =

_____

Come across (sth/sb) (phrasal verb) =

_____

Pitch dark (collocation) = _____

Turn (sth) on (phrasal verb) = _____

A scaredy cat (idiom) = _____

Cut (sth) up (phrasal verb) = _____

Pour (sth) in (phrasal verb) = _____

Turn (sth) off (phrasal verb) = _____

Turn up (phrasal verb) _____

Turn (sb/sth) down (phrasal verb) = _____

Turn (sb) off (phrasal verb) = _____

Call in on (sb) (phrasal verb) = _____

Figure (sth) out (phrasal verb) = _____

Turn out (phrasal verb) = _____

Turn into (phrasal verb) = _____

Exercise 15.1 🎧 29

Listen to text n. 1 while following along from text 2.

Exercise 15.2 🎧 30

Listen to text n. 2 while following along from text 1.

Exercise 15.3

Read the two texts, and complete the phrasal verbs and idiomatic expressions with their meaning.

Exercise 15.4

Listen to text n. 1 again, press pause after each sentence, and repeat.

Exercise 15.5

Put the correct preposition or particle next to the verb "TURN", choosing among: AROUND, AWAY, DOWN, ON, OFF (x2), OUT, UP, TO, INTO.

TURN AROUND	TURN ON	TURN UP
TURN AWAY	TURN OFF (x2)	TURN TO
TURN DOWN (x2)	TURN OUT	TURN INTO

1) Three years ago John was the shortest in his class. Now he has _____ (transformed himself/become) a giant. He's so tall!

2) The boys were _____ (refused admittance) from the disco club because they were underage.

3) He heard her voice. He _____ (turned himself in the opposite direction) and he saw her. She was smiling at him.

4) It's so dark in here. Please, _____ (switch on) the light.

5) Paul invited all of his classmates to the party, but some of them _____ him _____ (rejected his invitation).

6) They were ready to buy the car, but they were _____ (caused to lose interest) by some incongruous fine print in the contract.

7) My children always forget to _____ (switch off) the lights whenever they aren't in a room.

8) It _____ (happened) that the murderer wasn't the butler, as initially suspected, but the governess. Sorry for spoiling the ending of the book.

9) Jack didn't _____ (appear unexpectedly) until 11 pm, which annoyed everyone.

10) In the book, the protagonist is in dire straits (extreme difficulty) and although she _____ (has recourse to) other women for help, they suspiciously _____ her _____ (reject).

Exercise 15.6

Put the correct preposition or particle next to the verb "TURN", choosing among: AROUND, AWAY, DOWN, ON, OFF (x2), OUT, UP, TO, INTO.

1) They wanted to go to Croatia to spend the weekend at the beach, but when they arrived at the border control, they were turned _____ because one of them had forgotten his passport. So they had to turn _____ and drive back home.

2) Oh no! We left the ice-cream out for too long. Now it has turned _____ a warm syrup!

3) Whenever she has any doubts about cooking, she knows she can turn _____ her grandmother.

4) Andrew always turns the radio _____ when driving. He likes listening to music in his car.

5) Why did you turn _____ the lights when we left? Now we can't find the keys to the door.

6) Mike applied for the post of marketing manager, but he was turned _____ as they found someone more suitable for the position.

7) Non-constructive criticism can turn _____ anyone's enthusiasm.

8) When Christine went to Ireland, she met another young lady from Italy. It turned _____ that they lived three miles (five kilometers) from each other in Italy, but they had never met.

9) Paul turned _____ around lunchtime, and although unexpected, his aunt put together a nice meal for him.

Exercise 15.7

Complete the sentences with the following phrasal verbs:
End up, Sort out, Come across, Cut up, Pour in, Call in on, Figure out

1) Yesterday I _____ (found by chance) a pair of socks, which were hidden in a plant. How they _____ (finished) there, I have no idea!

2) Did you _____ (solve) the problem with your computer?

3) Unfortunately, we still haven't _____ (understood) what the problem with the computer is.

4) Jane _____ (cut in small pieces) her son's steak and _____ (put liquid) some orange juice _____ his glass for him.

5) Perhaps when we go to Italy we can _____ (pay a quick visit) my elderly cousin. She might be happy to see us.

Exercise 15.8

Complete the text with the following phrasal verbs:

End up, Sort out, Come across, Cut up, Pour in, Call in on, Figure out (x2).

1985. Mary was utterly perplexed by her sister's words this morning when she had briefly
1) _____ her. She really couldn't 2) _____ the meaning of her enigmatic words...
Was she angry? She wasn't aware that there had been something to 3) _____ between
them... She 4) _____ her apple, put it in her yogurt, and 5) _____ some coffee
_____ a cup, but she didn't 6) _____ finishing her breakfast. When she went out, she
7) _____ her best friend. Same mysterious hints: "6:00 o'clock. Tonight. We'll talk about
it then." She spent the whole day trying to 8) _____ what both her sister and her friend
could want... When she went to her sister's house, she found them both there. Silent. Serious. They
handed out an envelope to her. She opened it. As she opened it, the girls burst into laughter and
hugged her! They had found three tickets for the concert of Live Aid!

Exercise 15.9

Complete the sentences using: Phrasal Verbs with TURN + AROUND, AWAY,
DOWN, ON, OFF (x2), OUT, UP, TO, INTO and *End up, Sort out, Come across, Cut up, Pour in, Call in on,
Figure out*.

1) She heard a loud noise behind her, so she _____ to see what had happened.

2) Jane _____ the potatoes and put them in with the rest of the soup.

3) We didn't know how to _____ the problem of the transport to get to the airport, so we _____ calling a taxi.

4) In the fifties, men wearing long hair were _____ from restaurants as they were considered inappropriate.

5) Who _____ the TV _____ ? I was pretty sure I had _____ it _____ .

6) None of us could _____ the solution to the riddle. It _____ to be a really simple one.

7) Unfortunately, we have to _____ your kind invitation to dinner as we have a prior commitment on that day.

8) When Laura has a problem, she always _____ her older sister for advice. She knows she can always count on her.

9) Jack always _____ us at the strangest moments, which is a pity, because most of the time he _____ right when we are about to leave.

10) Paul _____ an old schoolmate of his the other day. She had _____ such a beautiful woman that he had hardly recognized her.

11) She _____ some herbal tea and sat on the sofa reading a nice book.

12) He was considering undergoing the surgery to his feet, but then he was _____ by the many side-effects. So, he decided against it.

Exercise 15.10

Look at Text 1 and write these sentences using an idiom, a phrase, or a collocation:

WITH A HEAVY HEART   A DOG'S LIFE

IT'S WATER UNDER THE BRIDGE   A SCAREDY CAT

IN ONE PIECE   PITCH DARK

1) My neighbor is a good man, but he leads a life full of hardship and little satisfaction.

_____

_____

2) My grandfather fought in the Second World War. Fortunately, he managed to come back home unharmed.

_____

_____

3) Many students go back to school after summer vacation <u>with lots of sadness.</u>

_____

4) You'll never convince her to sleep in a tent. She's <u>easily scared of everything.</u>

_____

5) Paul and Jack had a fight over something. But now they're friends again. <u>It doesn't matter any more.</u>

_____

_____

6) We need to replace the light bulb in the porch. It's <u>extremely dark</u> since it has burnt out.

_____

Suggestions for further practice

1) At the end of the chapter, play Text 2. Pause after each sentence, and re-tell the sentence using a phrasal verb or idiomatic expression. Check your answers from Text 1.

2) Try and re-tell the story using as many phrasal verbs and idiomatic expressions as you can remember.

3) After you have completed the exercises, erase your answers and do them again.

4) Write your own examples using the language items you have learned at the end of each chapter.

SOLUTIONS

CHAPTER 1

- Be well off (phrase) = be wealthy
- Be over (phrasal verb) = end
- Look for (phrasal verb) = search
- Take (sb) on (phrasal verb) = hire, recruit someone
- Look after (phrasal verb) = take care of
- Be away (phrasal verb) = be absent
- Be off (phrasal verb) = leave
- Be back (phrasal verb) = return
- Be in (phrasal verb) = be present
- Be up (phrasal verb) = be awake
- Be up to (sth) (phrasal verb) = try and do something, generally not good
- Be up to (sb) (phrasal verb) = decide
- Take (sth) on (phrasal verb) = accept a job or a responsibility
- Be in sb's shoes (idiom) = imagine being someone else

Exercise 1.5

1) Isn't in
2) Be over
3) Was up
4) Is up to
5) Am off; Be away; Be back
6) Is up to

Exercise 1.6

1) Back; Away; In
2) Up; Over
3) Off
4) Up to
5) Up to

Exercise 1.7

1) Look after

2) Take on

3) Looking for

4) Taking on

Exercise 1.8

1) Look after

2) Taken on

3) Looking for

4) Take on

Exercise 1.9

1) Looking for; Isn't in; Be back

2) Is...up to

3) A) Look after; Are away; Be off...; B) Take on; A) Is up to

4) A) Are... up; B) Is over; Take... on

Exercise 1.10

1) Were in my shoes

2) Well off

CHAPTER 2

- Break down (1) (phrasal verb) = burst into tears
- Call in (sick) (phrasal verb) = call a place (school, work) saying that you are sick
- Break out (phrasal verb) = develop a sudden rash
- Life isn't all roses (idiom) = life is hard
- Break into (phrasal verb) = forcefully enter somewhere
- Break (sth) off (phrasal verb) = interrupt something (here, a vacation)
- Go back (phrasal verb) = return
- Break up (phrasal verb) = end a relationship
- Have your heart broken (idiom) = feel really sad
- Break sb's heart (idiom) = make someone very sad
- Break down (2) (phrasal verb) = stop working
- Every cloud has a silver lining (idiom) = every negative event has something positive to it
- Give up (phrasal verb) = quit

- Take (sb) on (phrasal verb) = hire, recruit someone
- The cherry on top (AmE)/ The cherry on top of the cake (BrE) (idiom) = best of all

Exercise 2.5

1) Broke out
2) Break off
3) Broken up
4) Break into
5) Broke down
6) Break down

Exercise 2.6

1) Out; Off
2) Down
3) Up; Down
4) Into; Off

Exercise 2.7

1) Call in
2) Take... on
3) Go back
4) Gave... up

Exercise 2.8

1) Go back
2) Give up
3) Take.... On
4) Call in

Exercise 2.9

1) Breaking.... off
2) Break up; Give up
3) Broke down
4) Broke down; Break into; Called in
5) Broke out
6) Taking on

Exercise 2.10

1) Broke my heart
2) Every cloud has a silver lining
3) Life wasn't always all roses
4) The cherry on top was that...

CHAPTER 3

- Be as healthy as an ox (AmE)/ horse (BrE) (Idiom) = very healthy
- Act up (phrasal verb) = behave in an unusual way
- Call (sb) up (phrasal verb) = phone someone (BrE)/ call someone on the phone (AmE)
- Call (sb) back (phrasal verb) = call in return
- Call for (sth) (phrasal verb) = require
- Call (sth) off (phrasal verb) = cancel
- Call in on (sb) (phrasal verb) = go for a short visit
- Go in (phrasal verb) = enter
- State-of-the-art (phrase) = really modern and sophisticated
- Get through to (sb) (phrasal verb) = contact someone on the phone
- Get rid of (sth) (phrasal verb) = throw away
- Look forward to (sth) (phrasal verb) = feel excited about something

Exercise 3.5

1) Call off
2) Call in on
3) Calls for
4) Calling... up; Calls... back

Exercise 3.6

1) In on
2) Off
3) For
4) Up
5) Back

Exercise 3.7

1) Get rid of
2) Acting up

3) Get through to

4) Went in

5) Looking forward to

Exercise 3.8

1) Get rid of

2) Acting up

3) Go in

4) Looking forward to

5) Get through to

Exercise 3.9

1) Call... off

2) Acting up

3) Called for

4) Call... up; Get through to; Go in

5) Call in on

6) Call... back

7) Getting rid of

Exercise 3.10

1) As healthy as an ox

2) State-of-the-art

CHAPTER 4

- Come back (phrasal verb) = return
- Cross (sth) out (phrasal verb) = erase
- Carry (sth) out (phrasal verb) = perform, execute
- Carry (sth) off (phrasal verb) = execute successfully
- Carry (sth) around (phrasal verb) = transport something around
- Take away (phrasal verb) = take/ move someone/something from one place to another
- Pass away (phrasal verb) = die
- Give (sb) the shivers (idiom) = make someone feel scared
- Vanish into thin air (idiom) = disappear
- Carry (sb) back (to sth) (phrasal verb) = bring memories back (to someone's mind)
- Get down to (sth) (phrasal verb) = concentrate on something
- Get over (sth) (phrasal verb) = recover and continue

- Carry on (with sth) (phrasal verb) = continue
- Call in on (sb) (phrasal verb) = briefly visit
- Be over the moon (idiom) = be very happy

Exercise 4.5

1) Carried back

2) Carrying out; Carrying off

3) Carry on

4) Carrying around

Exercise 4.6

1) Back

2) On

3) Off

4) Around

5) Out

Exercise 4.7

1) Come back

2) Passed away

3) Take... away

4) Get down to

5) Cross ... out

6) Get over

7) Call in on

Exercise 4.8

1) Cross out

2) Get down to

3) Take.... away

4) Come back

5) Getting over

6) Passed away

7) Call in on

Exercise 4.9

1) Passed away; Get over; Carry on

2) Taken away

3) Cross out

4) Get down to

5) Came back; Carrying around

6) Carried out

7) Carried ... off

8) Call in on

Exercise 4.10

1) Vanished into thin air

2) Over the moon

3) Gives me the shivers

CHAPTER 5

- Come into (sth) (phrasal verb) = inherit
- Come apart (phrasal verb) = be broken into pieces
- Come about (phrasal verb) = occur, happen
- Break down (phrasal verb) = burst into tears
- Out of the blue (idiom) = out of nowhere; suddenly and unexpectedly
- Cheer (sb) up (phrasal verb) = uplift someone's mood
- Be down in the dumps (idiom) = be depressed
- Come up with (an idea) (phrasal verb) = have an idea/ create something new
- Come round to (sth) (phrasal verb) = change one's mind
- With the wave of the magic wand (idiom) = with the help of (the magic wand, a finger, an orchestra baton)
- Turn (sth/sb) into (phrasal verb) = transform
- Come across (sth) (phrasal verb) = find something or meet someone by chance
- Break the spell (idiom) = cease the effect of a magic spell
- At the stroke of (idiom) = exactly at a certain time
- Wake up (phrasal verb) = awake
- Get up (phrasal verb) = get out of bed
- Be sound asleep (phrase) = be in a deep sleep
- Come round/ come over (phrasal verb) = come for a visit

Exercise 5.5

1) Come about

2) Came across

3) Come round to

4) Come up with

5) Coming apart

6) Come round/come over

7) Came into

Exercise 5.6

1) Across

2) Apart

3) Round to

4) Round/ Over; Up with

5) Into

6) About

Exercise 5.7

1) Wake... up/ Get up

2) Broke down

3) Broke down/ Cheer... up

4) Turned ... into

5) Coming round/over

Exercise 5.8

1) Woke up

2) Got up

3) Coming over

4) Turned into

5) Come round

6) Broken down

7) Cheered... up

Exercise 5.9

1) Come apart

2) Came round to

3) Has come over/round

4) Cheer ... up

5) Came across

6) Break down

7) Woke .... Up

8) Turned into; Came into

9) Got up; Come about

Exercise 5.10

1) With the wave of

2) Broke the spell

3) Down in the dumps

4) At the stroke of

5) Sound asleep; Out of the blue

CHAPTER 6

- The straw that broke the camel's back (idiom) = the last of a series of events that makes you lose your patience
- Fall apart (1) (phrasal verb) = be broken, disintegrating, or in very bad condition
- Take (sb) on (phrasal verb) = hire, recruit someone
- Come up with (an idea) (phrasal verb) = have an idea
- Fall out (with sb) (phrasal verb) = quarrel with someone
- Fall for (phrasal verb) = believe something false to be true
- Give the green light (idiom) = agree on something, give one's approval or permission to do something (an idea, a project, etc.)
- Fall behind (schedule) (phrasal verb) = fail to meet the scheduled deadlines
- Bring about (phrasal verb) = cause
- It's like talking to a brick wall (idiom) = talking to someone who won't listen
- Utterly frustrating (collocation) = terribly frustrating
- Fall apart (2) (phrasal verb) = have a nervous breakdown
- (Not) be worth it (idiom) = (not) be worth the effort/ (not) be valuable enough to dedicate time and energy to someone or something
- Fall back on (sth) (phrasal verb) = have recourse to
- Carry out (phrasal verb) = complete a task
- Fall through (phrasal verb) = fail/ not be successful
- Keep one's spirits high/up (idiom) = remain optimistic
- Play it by ear (idiom) = deal with a situation day by day
- Figure (sth) out (phrasal verb) = understand something/ find a solution to a problem

Exercise 6.5

1) Falling apart
2) Fell through
3) Fall for
4) Falling behind
5) Fell out
6) Fall back on
7) Fell apart

Exercise 6.6

1) Through
2) For
3) Out
4) Behind
5) Through; Back on
6) Apart

Exercise 6.7

1) Brought about
2) Come up with; Figure ... out
3) Take on
4) Carries out

Exercise 6.8

1) Brought about
2) Take ... on
3) Carrying out
4) Figuring ... out
5) Came up with

Exercise 6.9

1) Falling apart; Figure ... out
2) Coming up with; Fall back on
3) Brought about
4) Carrying out; Fall behind
5) Carries out; Take... on; Fall apart
6) Figure... out
7) Fell out; Fell through

Exercise 6.10

1) Play it by ear

2) That was the last straw that broke the camel's back

3) Keep your spirits high

4) Utterly frustrating; Is like a brick wall

5) It wasn't worth it

6) Gave him the green light

CHAPTER 7

- A bright young thing (idiom) = young and enthusiastic
- Get on/along with (sb) (phrasal verb) = be friends with a person and share the same ideas
- Heavy-hearted (collocation) = quite sad and thoughtful
- Drop in (phrasal verb) = go for a visit
- A storm is brewing (idiom) = trouble or a negative situation is about to happen or developing with potential negative consequences
- Drop out (of school) (phrasal verb) = leave school
- Not believe one's (own) ears (idiom) = be extremely surprised
- Go through (trouble) (phrasal verb) = have problems (or a difficult period)
- Come down on (sb) (phrasal verb) = rebuke someone very harshly
- Get over (sth) (phrasal verb) = overcome something
- Call in (sick) (phrasal verb) = call a place (school, work) saying that you are sick
- Talk (sb) out (of sth) (phrasal verb) = try and convince a person not to do something
- Get (sth) across (to sb) (phrasal verb) = make someone understand something
- Storm (at sb) (idiom) = address someone very angrily and aggressively
- Get away with (sth) (phrasal verb) = go unpunished
- That's final! (phrase) = that's the final decision/ definitive
- Sth makes one's blood boil (idiom) = make someone feel furious and indignant over something
- See eye to eye with sb (idiom) = entirely agree with someone
- Get away (from sth) (phrasal verb) = avoid
- Join forces (collocation) = gather together (to achieve a common goal)
- Get through to (sb) (phrasal verb) = contact someone
- Get rid of (sth/sb) (phrasal verb) = dispose of something/someone
- Help (sb) out (phrasal verb) = help
- Be in (phrase) = accept to be part of a project

- Get down to (work, studying, etc.) (phrasal verb) = start (studying, working on..)
- Get through (phrasal verb) = pass through something
- Pass with flying colors (idiom) = pass with honors (successfully)
- A tempest in a teapot (AmE)/ A storm in a teacup (BrE) (idiom) = a big deal over nothing/ excessive excitement over nothing

Exercise 7.5

1) Get over
2) Get rid of
3) Get on/along
4) Gets through; Gets away with
5) Get down to
6) Get through to
7) Get away from
8) Get across to

Exercise 7.6

1) Across to
2) Rid of
3) Down to; Through
4) Through to
5) Away with; Rid of
6) Away from
7) On/along
8) Over

Exercise 7.7

1) Dropped in
2) Called in
3) Went through
4) Came down on; Talk ... out of
5) Dropping out
6) Help ... out; Is in

Exercise 7.8

1) Dropped in
2) Came down on

3) Going through

4) Called in

5) Drop out

6) Talk ... out

7) Help ... out

8) Am in

Exercise 7.9

1) Went through; Call in; Get over

2) Came down (on); Get rid of; Talk ... out (of)

3) Dropped out

4) Get through to

5) Got down to; Got through

6) Dropped in; Get on/along

7) Got away with

8) Get away from

9) Are... in?

10) Help... out

Exercise 7.10

1) Passed his test with flying colors; I couldn't believe my ears

2) See eye to eye; Storm at you

3) Heavy-hearted; A bright young thing; Join forces

4) A storm is brewing

5) A storm was brewing

6) A tempest in a teapot

7) Made Paul's blood boil

8) I'm in!

CHAPTER 8

- Go on at (sb) (phrasal verb) (BrE) = repeatedly criticize
- Take up (a new interest) (phrasal verb) = pursue (a new interest)
- Cross the line (idiom) = exaggerate
- A glimmer of hope (collocation) = a small sign of improvement
- Go in for (sth) (phrasal verb) = undertake
- Go over (sth) (phrasal verb) = examine

- Go off (phrasal verb) = explode
- Go out of (a place) (phrasal verb) = exit (a place)
- Go back (phrasal verb) = return
- Go after (sb) (phrasal verb) = chase (someone)
- Go back on (a decision, a choice) (phrasal verb) = change one's mind
- Put sb/ Be in a tough spot (idiom) = put someone in a difficult situation
- Go on (phrasal verb) = continue
- Face the music (idiom) = face the consequences of a choice
- Go down (phrasal verb) = diminish, decrease
- Go off the beaten path (idiom) = step out of the conventional path

Exercise 8.5

1) Went over
2) Gone down
3) Went off
4) Go on
5) Went out of
6) Going on at; Go back on
7) Go back; Go in for
8) Going after

Exercise 8.6

1) Off
2) On at
3) Out of; Down; Back
4) Over
5) Back on
6) On
7) After
8) In for

Exercise 8.7

1) Went in for; Went back on; Took up
2) Go down; Go on
3) Taken up; Go out of
4) Went over; Go on at

5) Went after

6) Go back

Exercise 8.8

1) Took up

2) Going in for

3) Going back on

4) Go on

5) Going after

6) Going back

7) Go out of

8) Went down

9) Went over

Exercise 8.9

1) Go off the beaten path

2) Put someone in a tough spot

3) Crossed the line; Face the music

4) A glimmer of hope

CHAPTER 9

- Feel on edge (idiom) = feel extremely nervous

- Hand (sth) out (phrasal verb) = distribute something (by hand)

- Be kept back (phrasal verb) (AmE) = be retained/ be held back

- Ace a test/ a job interview (idiom) = pass with a high score

- Well up with tears (idiom) = eyes starting to fill with tears

- Keep (sth) in (phrasal verb) = restrain oneself

- Cut the air with a knife (idiom) = tension that can be tangibly felt

- Breathe (sth) in (phrasal verb) = inhale

- Breathe (sth) out (phrasal verb) = exhale

- Keep (sth) down (phrasal verb) = be quiet/ not make any noise

- Keep to (sth) (phrasal verb) = follow (rules, directions, etc.)

- Keep off (sth) (phrasal verb) = avoid something

- Keep up with (sth) (phrasal verb) = keep pace with (something/someone)

- Hand (sth) in (phrasal verb) = give something to an authority (teacher, police officer, etc.)

- Get started (phrase) = begin

- Put on one's thinking cap (idiom) = think about something seriously and with focus
- A race against time (idiom) = not have enough time
- Keep on (+ ing) (phrasal verb) = continue
- Turn out (phrasal verb) = happen unexpectedly
- Nail something (idiom) = go very well
- The cherry on top (AmE)/ The cherry on top of the cake (BrE) (idiom) = on top of that
- Carry (sth) off (phrasal verb) = pass (execute) something successfully
- Fall behind with (sth) (phrasal verb) = fail to meet deadlines
- Run things like clockwork (idiom) = manage things in a timely and well-organized manner

Exercise 9.5

1) Keep up with
2) Keep off
3) Keep to
4) Kept back
5) Keep .... Down; Kept on
6) Keeps ... in

Exercise 9.6

1) Down
2) To; On; Off
3) Back
4) Up with; In

Exercise 9.7

1) Hand out
2) Turned out; Fallen behind with
3) Breathe in; Breathe ... out
4) Handed in

Exercise 9.8

1) Handed out
2) Fallen behind with
3) Breathed in
4) Breathed out
5) Handed in
6) Turned out

Exercise 9.10

1) Breathe in; Breathe out

2) Keeps on; Keep up with

3) Keep off

4) Keep ..... down

5) Handed out; Kept... in; Turned out

6) Fell ... behind with; Kept back

Exercise 9.11

1) The cherry on top

2) Put on your thinking cap

3) Get started

4) Runs things like clockwork

5) Well up with tears

6) Cut the air with a knife

7) Felt on edge; Nailed everything and aced the test

8) It was a race against time/ We raced against time

CHAPTER 10

- Look back on (sth) (phrasal verb) = remember
- Look down on (sth/sb) (phrasal verb) = treat (or think of) something/someone poorly
- Blow (sth) up (phrasal verb) = explode
- Look on (sth/sb) (phrasal verb) = regard (something/someone)
- It's a piece of cake (idiom) = it's easy
- Look out (phrasal verb) = beware of something
- Look out for (sth/sb) = pay close attention to something specific
- Tender age (collocation) = in younger years
- (Be) Green with envy (idiom) = be envious
- (Be) at a turning point (phrase) = a time of decisive change
- Pass by/ Go by (phrasal verb) = elapse
- Go down (phrasal verb) = decrease
- Be the salt of the earth (idiom) = be good and honest people
- Train of thought (phrase) = a series of thoughts
- Look (sth) over (phrasal verb) = examine something quickly
- Catch one's eye (idiom) = catch someone's attention

- Look through (sth) (phrasal verb) = search
- Figure (sth) out (phrasal verb) = understand
- Weigh all the pros and cons (phrase) = ponder all the positive and negative aspects
- Be in a tight spot (idiom) = be in a difficult position
- Be torn (idiom) = be undecided (between two things)
- Look forward to (sth) (phrasal verb) = wait in anticipation
- Be at stake (idiom) = be liable to be lost, at risk
- Jump in (phrasal verb) = take action enthusiastically (often without thinking enough)
- Phase in (phrasal verb) = introduce oneself into a new phase gradually

Exercise 10.5

1) Looking down on
2) Look out
3) Looked over
4) Look out for
5) Looked back on
6) Looked through
7) Looking forward to
8) Looked on

Exercise 10.6

1) Down on
2) On
3) Back on
4) Over
5) Out
6) Through
7) Out for
8) Forward to

Exercise 10.7

1) Figure out; Blow up
2) Jump …. into
3) Passed by/Went by
4) Phased … in
5) Go down

Exercise 10.8

1) Blew up

2) Go by/pass by

3) Figure out

4) Jump in

5) Gone down

6) Phase .... in

Exercise 10.9

1) Look out; Blow up

2) Looked through

3) Looked back on

4) Look down on

5) Looked over

6) Look out for; Gone down

7) Look on

8) Jumping into; Figure out

9) Phased in

10) Goes by/ passes by

11) Looking forward to

Exercise 10.10

1) The salt of the earth

2) In a tight spot; Torn; Weigh the pros and cons; A piece of cake

3) At stake

4) Tender age

5) She was at a turning point

6) Green with envy

7) Caught her eye; Train of thought

CHAPTER 11

- Save (sth) up (phrasal verb) = set money aside

- Be made up of (phrasal verb) = be composed of

- Have the time of one's life (idiom) = have lots of fun

- Be on cloud nine (idiom) = be elated, extremely happy

- Make of (sth) (phrasal verb) = form an idea about something

- Crack jokes (idiom) = tell jokes
- Roar with laughter (collocation) = laugh heartily
- Make for (phrasal verb) = go into a specific direction
- Make (sth/sb) out (phrasal verb) = understand
- Not put much thought into something (phrase) = not pay much attention to something
- Make up (sth) (1) (phrasal verb) = invent an excuse
- Memories came flooding back (phrase) = memories suddenly come back
- Pass out (phrasal verb) = faint
- Pass away (phrasal verb) = die
- Out of the blue (idiom) = all of a sudden
- Act weird (phrase) = behave differently
- Look/be/feel blue (idiom) = look/be/feel sad
- Make (sth) up (2) (phrasal verb) = create something
- Cheer (sb) up (phrasal verb) = try and make someone happy
- Have a rush of memories (phrase) = a sudden and powerful recollection of memories
- Take it easy (idiom) = relax
- Make up with (sth/sb) (phrasal verb) = make peace with (something/someone)
- Cool (sth/sb) off (phrasal verb) = refresh something/oneself
- Make up for (sth) (phrasal verb) = compensate for something
- Be as good as new (idiom) = be in very good condition
- Be at the wheel (idiom) = drive
- Make (sth) up (to sb) (phrasal verb) = compensate for something to someone
- A trip/a walk down memory lane (idiom) = time spent recollecting past memories

Exercise 11.5

1) Made up of
2) Make of
3) Make .... up
4) Make up for
5) Make out
6) Made for
7) Made up
8) Made up with
9) Make .... up to

Exercise 11.6

1) For
2) Up
3) For; Up of
4) Up
5) Of
6) Out
7) Up for
8) Up to
9) Up with; Up to

Exercise 11.7

1) Cool off
2) Passed away; cheer... up
3) Passed out
4) Saving up

Exercise 11.8

1) Passed away
2) Passed out
3) Saving up
4) Cool ... off
5) Cheer ... up

Exercise 11.9

1) Made for; Cool off
2) Passed out; Cool....off
3) Make up for
4) Cheer up; Makes up with
5) Make of; Pass away
6) Made up; Make... up to
7) Made up
8) Make out; Saved up
9) Made up of

Exercise 11.10

1) Take it easy; Cracks jokes; Roar with laughter

2) Feel blue; Is as good as new

3) On cloud nine; Be at the wheel

4) Memories came flooding back

5) A rush of memories

6) The time of our lives; Trips down memory lane

7) Didn't put much thought into

8) Acting weird

9) Out of the blue

CHAPTER 12

- Be on top of the world (Idiom) = be thrilled/ extremely happy

- Put (sth) up (phrasal verb) = build

- A once-in-a-lifetime opportunity (collocation) = a very special opportunity

- All but = all except

- Smooth sailing (idiom) = easy

- Open a can of worms (idiom) = find a lot of problems

- Put (sb) through to (sb) (phrasal verb) = connect someone on the phone

- A tough nut to crack (idiom) = tough, difficult

- Put (sth) back/ off (or Push sth back) (phrasal verb) = postpone

- Put (sth) forward (or Bring sth forward) (phrasal verb) = move at an earlier date or time

- Put (sth) down to (phrasal verb) = attribute the cause to

- Go the extra mile (idiom) = exceed one's expectations, make an effort

- Put up with (sth) (phrasal verb) = tolerate

- Catch one's breath (idiom) = rest a bit

- Call (sb) up (phrasal verb) = call someone on the phone

- Put (sb) up (phrasal verb) = host someone

- Lend a sympathetic ear (phrase) = listen with sympathy

- Put (sb) down (phrasal verb) = belittle someone

- Put (sb) off (phrasal verb) = demoralize

- Put (sth) on (1) (phrasal verb) = wear some items of clothing

- Put (sth) on (2) (phrasal verb) = turn the lights on

- Put (sth) out (1) (phrasal verb) = turn the lights off

- Burn (sth) out (phrasal verb) = cease to burn

- Put (sth) out (2) (phrasal verb) = extinguish (a source of fire)
- The end is in sight (phrase) = the end is near
- Grin and bear it (idiom) = resist, endure the difficulties without complaining, stoically
- Pay off the effort (idiom) = meet someone's efforts with a successful outcome
- Pay (sth) off (phrasal verb) = pay a debt/mortgage etc. in full
- A bumpy ride (idiom) = a hard time
- Turn out (phrasal verb) = reveal itself
- A blessing in disguise (idiom) = something positive after seeming negative

Exercise 12.5

1) Put forward
2) Put ... down to
3) Put out
4) Put on; Put... out
5) Put up
6) Put on
7) Put .... down
8) Put back/off
9) Put ... through to
10) Put off
11) Put up with
12) Put... up

Exercise 12.6

1) Up with
2) Through to
3) Out
4) Down
5) Off
6) On
7) On; Out
8) Up
9) Down to
10) Back/off
11) Forward
12) Up

Exercise 12.7

1) Paid off
2) Turn off
3) Called... up
4) Turned on
5) Turned out
6) Burn out

Exercise 12.8

1) Paid off
2) Called up
3) Turned out
4) Turn off
5) Turned ... on

Exercise 12.9

1) Turn on; put on
2) Turn off ; put out
3) Put.. off; Putting up; Paid off
4) Put back/off
5) Put forward; Bring forward
6) Put... down; Put.... down to; Put up with; Turned out
7) Put out
8) Put... through to
9) Called ... up
10) Put ... up

Exercise 12.10

1) Catch my breath
2) It opened a can of worms
3) A tough nut to crack
4) A bumpy ride; A blessing in disguise
5) Smooth sailing
6) Goes the extra mile
7) Lend a sympathetic ear
8) The end was in sight; On top of the world; Paid off his effort

9) A one-in-a-lifetime opportunity

10) Grin and bear it

CHAPTER 13

- Be on in years (idiom) = be not so young any more
- Set (sb) apart from (phrasal verb) = be different from other people
- Run after (sth/sb) (phrasal verb) = persistently pursue (something, someone)
- Not sweat sth (phrase) = not worry over something
- Run over (sth) (phrasal verb) = quickly read, revise something
- Set about (sth) (phrasal verb) = start doing something/dealing with something
- Set (sb/sth) back (phrasal verb) = delay
- Have a vivid imagination (collocation) = be imaginative
- Run out of (sth) (phrasal verb) = finish one's supply of something
- Set (sth) out (phrasal verb) = write down something clearly and in a detailed way
- Have an ace up one's sleeve (idiom) = have a secret resource
- Be down to earth (idiom) = be practical, unpretentious
- Run (sth) by (sb) (phrasal verb) = tell your ideas to someone (to ask for their opinion)
- Be the apple of one's eye (idiom) = be someone's favorite
- Be green with envy (idiom) = be envious
- Run (sb/sth) over (phrasal verb) = hit someone/something with a vehicle
- Set (sb/sth) on (sb) (phrasal verb) = attack someone/something
- Run into (sth) (phrasal verb) = experience something (generally difficult)
- Be a good egg (idiom) = be a good person
- Be a smart cookie (idiom) = be intelligent
- Run into (sb) (phrasal verb) = meet someone by chance
- Set out/off (phrasal verb) = leave
- Set (sth) off (phrasal verb) = have something explode
- Set (sth) up (phrasal verb) = establish
- Be the salt of the earth (idiom) = be a fine and noble person

Exercise 13.5

1) Ran out of

2) Ran over

3) Ran into

4) Ran into; Run by

5) Ran after

6) Ran over

Exercise 13.6

1) Into

2) After; Over; Into

3) By

4) Out of

5) Over

Exercise 13.7

1) Set out/off

2) Set ... on

3) Set about; Set back

4) Sets... apart; Set up

5) Set off

6) Set off

7) Set out

Exercise 13.8

1) Back

2) Out/ Off

3) Apart

4) On

5) About

6) Up

7) Off

8) Out

Exercise 13.9

1) Set out/off; Ran into; Set...back

2) Ran after; Set...on

3) Run over

4) Ran over

5) Set off

6) Ran out of

7) Set about; Setting out

8) Run…. by

9) Ran into; Set up; Sets … apart

Exercise 13.10

1) The salt of the earth

2) Good egg; Be green with envy

3) Vivid imagination; The ace up his sleeve

4) A smart cookie

5) Down to earth

6) Don't sweat it!

7) Getting on in years

CHAPTER 14

- Be like two peas in a pod (idiom) = extremely similar
- Take after (sb) (phrasal verb) = resemble someone
- Take (sth) back (1) (phrasal verb) = admit that one is wrong
- Be at fault (phrase) = make a mistake
- Take (sb) back (to the past) (phrasal verb) = have someone remember about the past
- Take a walk/trip down memory lane (idiom) = remember things from the past
- Grow up (phrasal verb) = become older/ become an adult
- Pass away (phrasal verb) = die
- Take (sb) in (phrasal verb) = take someone to live with you
- At an early age (phrase) = when someone was very young
- Turn out (phrasal verb) = reveal itself to be (good, etc.)
- Be in touch (phrase) = communicate by phone, e-mail, etc.
- Grow apart (phrasal verb) = stop being friends (become less close)
- Blood is thicker than water (proverb) = family bonds are extremely strong
- Unbeknownst to sb (phrase) = without someone knowing something
- Take up (sth) (phrasal verb) = start a new hobby or interest
- Try (sth) on (phrasal verb) = put some clothes on to see if they fit
- Take (sth) back (2) (phrasal verb) = return an item
- Take (sb) on (phrasal verb) = hire, recruit someone
- Take (time/days..) off (phrasal verb) = take a vacation
- Set off/out (phrasal verb) = leave
- Have butterflies in one's stomach (idiom) = be very nervous/excited

- Take off (plane) (1) (phrasal verb) = (of a plane) leave the ground
- Take (sth) off (phrasal verb) = remove one's clothes
- Find (sth) out (phrasal verb) = discover
- Take (sb) out (phrasal verb) = invite someone to go out together
- Laid-back (adjective) = relaxed
- Heartbreaking (adjective) = sad (saddening, emotionally difficult)
- Carry on (phrasal verb) = continue
- Not be growing any younger (phrase) = get old
- Immediate family (collocation) = close family members
- Take off (2) (phrasal verb) = improve
- Run a business/ a branch/ a store (collocation) = manage a business/branch/etc.
- Take (sth) on (phrasal verb) = accept (a job or a responsibility)
- Take to (sb/sth) (phrasal verb) = start liking someone/something
- Take a leap of faith (idiom) = make a decision despite all the uncertainties of the case
- Bear a striking resemblance to sb (phrase) = look very similar

Exercise 14.5

1) Took off
2) Takes on
3) Takes after
4) Took off
5) Take back
6) Took .... back
7) Take off
8) Took ... in
9) Took up
10) Took on
11) Took.... out
12) Takes ... back
13) Took to

Exercise 14.6

1) Off
2) After
3) On; Off: Out
4) In

5) Back

6) Up

7) To

8) Back

9) Off

10) On

11) Back

Exercise 14.7

1) Found out; Passed away; Grown apart

2) Grew up

3) Carry on

4) Turned out

5) Try ... on

6) Set off/out

Exercise 14.8

1) Grew up

2) Grew apart

3) Carried on

4) Passed away

5) Set off/ out

6) Trying on

7) Turned out

8) Found out

Exercise 14.9

1) Taken after; Turned out

2) Take... off; Try... on

3) Set off/out; Found out; Take off

4) Carry on

5) Grew apart; Grew up

6) Take ... back

7) Passed away

8) Took to; Took ... up

9) Took off; Taken on

10) Take on

11) Took .... back

12) Took ... in

13) Take ... out

Exercise 14.10

1) Bear a striking resemblance; Are like two peas in a pod

2) Unbeknownst to her

3) Taking a leap of faith

4) Running his company

5) Kept in touch; From an early age

6) Immediate family; Is at fault; Blood is thicker than water

7) Were getting on in years; Take a walk down memory lane

8) Butterflies in his stomach

CHAPTER 15

- Turn around (phrasal verb) = turn yourself in the opposite direction
- With a heavy heart (collocation) = with a sad heart
- Turn (sb) away (phrasal verb) = refuse someone admittance to a place
- End up (phrasal verb) = ultimately find oneself doing something
- It's water under the bridge (idiom) = it's not important any more
- Turn to (sb) (phrasal verb) = ask for help and assistance
- Sort (sth) out (phrasal verb) = solve a problem
- In one piece (idiom) = be unharmed
- A dog's life (idiom) = an unhappy existence full of difficulties
- Come across (sth/sb) (phrasal verb) = find/meet something/someone by chance
- Pitch dark (collocation) = completely dark
- Turn (sth) on (phrasal verb) = switch (something) on
- A scaredy cat (idiom) = a timid creature, easily scared by everything
- Cut (sth) up (phrasal verb) = cut (something) in little pieces
- Pour (sth) in (phrasal verb) = put some liquid into a container
- Turn (sth) off (phrasal verb) = switch (something) off
- Turn up (phrasal verb) = arrive unexpectedly
- Turn (sb/sth) down (phrasal verb) = to refuse (someone/something)
- Turn (sb) off (phrasal verb) = make (someone) lose interest in (something)

- Call in on (sb) (phrasal verb) = pay a short visit
- Figure (sth) out (phrasal verb) = understand
- Turn out (phrasal verb) = reveal itself, happen
- Turn into (sth) (phrasal verb) = transform

Exercise 15.5

1) Turned into

2) Turned away

3) Turned around

4) Turn on

5) Turned ... down

6) Turned off

7) Turn off

8) Turned out

9) Turn up

10) Turns to; Turn ... down

Exercise 15.6

1) Away; Around

2) Into

3) To

4) On

5) Off

6) Down

7) Off

8) Out

9) Up

Exercise 15.7

1) Came across; Ended up

2) Sort out

3) Figured out

4) Cut up; Poured ... in

5) Call in on

Exercise 15.8

1) Called in on
2) Figure out
3) Sort out
4) Cut up
5) Poured... in
6) End up
7) Came across
8) Figure out

Exercise 15.9

1) Turned around
2) Cut up
3) Sort out; Ended up
4) Turned away
5) Turned ... on; Turned... off
6) Figure out; Turned out
7) Turn down
8) Turns to
9) Calls in on; Turns up
10) Came across; Turned into
11) Poured in
12) Turned off

Exercise 15.10

1) A dog's life
2) In one piece
3) With a heavy heart
4) A scaredy cat
5) It's water under the bridge
6) Pitch dark

GLOSSARY

CHAPTER 1 - BE - AN UNEXPECTED OPPORTUNITY

Phrasal verb	Type	Meaning
Be away	Type 1 (Intransitive inseparable)	Be absent (generally out of town)
Be back	Type 3 (Transitive inseparable)	Return
Be in	Type 1 (Intransitive inseparable)	Be present (at home, or in a certain enclosed space)
Be off	Type 1 (Intransitive inseparable)	Leave a place
Be over	Type 3 (Transitive inseparable)	End, finish
Be up	Type 1 (Intransitive inseparable)	Be awake (not asleep)
Be up to (sb)	Type 4 (Transitive inseparable with two prepositions)	Decide something
Be up to (sth)	Type 4 (Transitive inseparable with two prepositions)	Try and do something unusual, secretive, generally not good
Look after	Type 3 (Transitive inseparable)	Take care of something/ someone
Look for	Type 3 (Transitive inseparable)	Search for something/someone
Take (sb) on	Type 2 (Transitive separable)	Hire, recruit someone
Take (sth) on	Type 2 (Transitive separable)	Accept a job or a responsibility

Idiom/ Phrase/ Collocation/ etc.	Meaning
Be/ Put oneself in sb's shoes (idiom)	Try to imagine being someone else
Be well off (phrase)	Be wealthy

CHAPTER 2 - BREAK - EVERY CLOUD HAS A SILVER LINING

Phrasal Verb	Type	Meaning
Break down (1)	Type 1 (Intransitive inseparable))	Burst into tears, start crying
Break down (2)	Type 1 (Intransitive inseparable)	Stop working, be broken (used for cars, buses, etc.)
Break into	Type 3 (Transitive inseparable)	Forcefully enter someone's property without permission, generally ill-intentioned
Break (sth) off	Type 2 (Transitive separable)	Interrupt something
Break out	Type 1 (Intransitive inseparable)	Erupt, start suddenly, violently and unexpectedly (ex. a war, a fight, a pandemic, a rash)
Break up	Type 1 (Intransitive inseparable)	End a relationship
Call in	Type 1 (Intransitive inseparable)	Call a place, especially the place where you work, to inform them about something (sickness, delay, etc.)
Give (sth) up	Type 2 (Transitive separable)	Quit something, stop doing something (generally because harmful)
Go back	Type 1 (Intransitive inseparable)	Return to a place
Take (sb) on	Type 2 (Transitive separable)	Hire, recruit someone

Idiom/ Phrase/ Collocation/etc.	Meaning
Break sb's heart (idiom)	Make someone feel extremely sad about something
Every cloud has a silver lining (idiom)	Every negative event brings something positive
Life isn't all roses (idiom)	Life is hard/ Life isn't always easy
The cherry on top (AmE)/ The cherry on top of the cake (BrE) (idiom)	Some extra bonus added to an already good situation (like the cherry on top of a cake)

CHAPTER 3 - CALL - GOOD GENES

Phrasal verb	Type	Meaning
Call (sb) back	Type 2 (Transitive separable)	Return a phone call
Call for (sth)	Type 3 (Transitive inseparable)	Require, need something (which is missing)
Call (sth) off	Type 2 (Transitive separable)	Cancel something (an arrangement, a meeting, an event, etc.)
Call in on (sb)	Type 4 (Transitive inseparable with two prepositions)	Go for a short visit
Call (sb) up	Type 2 (Transitive separable)	Phone someone (BrE)/ Call someone on the phone (AmE)
Act up	Type 1 (Intransitive inseparable)	Behave in an unusual way
Get rid of (sth)	Type 4 (Transitive inseparable with two prepositions)	Throw something away
Get through to (sb)	Type 4 (Transitive inseparable with two prepositions)	Contact someone on the phone
Go in	Type 1 (Intransitive inseparable)	Enter a place
Look forward to (sth)	Type 4 (Transitive inseparable with two prepositions)	Feel excited about something/ Wait with anticipation for something

Idiom/ Phrase/ Collocation/ etc.	Meaning
As healthy as an ox (AmE)/horse (BrE) (idiom)	Very healthy
State-of-the-art (phrase)	Really modern and sophisticated

CHAPTER 4 - CARRY - A SPECIAL FRIENDSHIP

Phrasal verb	Type	Meaning
Carry (sth) around	Type 2 (Transitive separable)	Transport something around

Phrasal verb	Type	Meaning
Carry (sb) back (to sth)	Type 2 (Transitive separable)	Bring memories back into someone's mind
Carry on (with sth)	Type 3 (Transitive inseparable)	Continue doing something
Carry (sth) out	Type 2 (Transitive separable)	Perform, effect, execute, complete (an experiment, an assignment, orders, etc.)
Carry (sth) off	Type 2 (Transitive separable)	Succeed in doing something difficult; execute, complete something perceived as difficult
Call in on (sb)	Type 4 (Transitive inseparable with two prepositions)	Go for a short visit
Come back	Type 3 (Transitive inseparable)	Return to a place
Cross (sth) out	Type 2 (Transitive separable)	Erase something with a line
Get down to (sth)	Type 4 (Transitive inseparable with two prepositions)	Concentrate on something
Get over (sth)	Type 3 (Transitive inseparable)	Overcome something, recover from something and continue one's life
Pass away	Type 1 (Intransitive inseparable)	Die
Take (sb/sth) away	Type 2 (Transitive separable)	Remove someone or something from a place and take them to another

Idiom/ Phrase/ Collocation/ etc.	Meaning
Be over the moon (idiom)	Be extremely happy
Give sb the shivers (idiom)	Make someone feel scared
Vanish into thin air (idiom)	Disappear

CHAPTER 5 - COME - AT THE STROKE OF MIDNIGHT

Phrasal verb	Type	Meaning
Come about	Type 1 (Intransitive inseparable)	Happen, occur
Come across (sb/sth)	Type 3 (Transitive inseparable)	Meet someone or find something by chance
Come apart	Type 1 (Intransitive inseparable)	Disintegrate, be broken into pieces
Come into (sth)	Type 3 (Transitive inseparable)	Inherit something
Come round/ over	Type 1 (Intransitive inseparable)	Come for a visit
Come round to (sth)	Type 4 (Transitive inseparable with two prepositions)	Change one's mind about something
Come up with (sth)	Type 4 (Transitive inseparable with two prepositions)	Create something/ have an idea/ find a creative solution
Break down	Type 1 (Intransitive inseparable)	Burst into tears, suddenly start to cry
Cheer (sb) up	Type 2 (Transitive separable)	Uplift someone's mood
Get up	Type 1 (Intransitive inseparable)	Leave someone's own bed and be ready for the day
Turn (sb/sth) into (sth)	Type 2 (Transitive separable)	Transform someone/something into someone/something else
Wake up Wake (sb) up	Type 1 (Intransitive inseparable) Type 2 (Transitive separable)	Cease to sleep; Cause someone to cease to sleep

Idiom/ Phrase /Collocation/ etc.	Meaning
At the stroke of (idiom)	Exactly at a certain time
Be down in the dumps (idiom)	Be extremely sad and depressed
Be sound asleep (phrase)	Sleep deeply
Break the spell (idiom)	Cease the effect of a magic spell, or a special moment
Out of the blue (idiom)	Suddenly and unexpectedly
With the wave of the magic wand (idiom)	With the help of (the magic wand, a finger, an orchestra baton, etc.)

CHAPTER 6 - FALL - KEEP YOUR SPIRITS HIGH!

Phrasal verb	Type	Meaning
Fall apart (1)	Type 1 (Intransitive inseparable)	Be broken, disintegrating, or in very bad condition
Fall apart (2)	Type 1 (Intransitive inseparable)	Have a nervous breakdown
Fall back on (sth)	Type 4 (Transitive inseparable with two prepositions)	Have recourse to something
Fall behind Fall behind (schedule)	Type 1 (Intransitive inseparable) Type 3 (Transitive inseparable)	Fail to finish work on time; fail to meet a deadline
Fall for (sb/sth)	Type 3 (Transitive inseparable)	1) Be tricked into believing something that was not true 2) Become infatuated with someone; to fall in love
Fall out (with sb/ over sth)	Type 3 (Transitive inseparable)	Have a serious argument with some-one and stop being friendly with them
Fall through	Type 1 (Intransitive inseparable)	Fail; not be successful
Bring about	Type 3 (Transitive inseparable)	Cause something to happen
Carry out	Type 2 (Transitive separable)	Perform, effect, execute, complete (an experiment, an assignment, orders, etc.)
Come up with	Type 4 (Transitive inseparable with two prepositions)	Create something/ have an idea/ find a creative solution
Figure (sth) out	Type 2 (Transitive separable)	Understand something/ find a solution to a problem
Take (sb) on	Type 2 (Transitive separable)	Hire, recruit someone

Idiom/ Phrase/ Collocation/ etc.	Meaning
(Not) Be worth it (idiom)	(Not) be valuable enough to dedicate time and energy to someone or something
Give the green light (idiom)	Agree on something, give one's approval or permission to do something (an idea, a project, etc.)

Idiom/ Phrase/ Collocation/ etc.	Meaning
It's like talking to a brick wall (idiom)	Talking to someone who won't listen, generally because very stubborn
Keep one's spirits high/up (idiom)	Remain optimistic
Play it by ear (idiom)	Deal with a situation day by day
The last straw that broke the camel's back (idiom)	The last of a series of events that make one lose their patience
Utterly frustrating (collocation)	Very frustrating

CHAPTER 7 - DROP/ GET - A TEMPEST IN A TEAPOT

Phrasal verb	Type	Meaning
Drop in	Type 1 (Intransitive inseparable)	Go for a visit
Drop out (of school)	Type 3 (Transitive inseparable)	Leave school or university before the academic year finishes
Get (sth) across (to sb)	Type 2 (Transitive separable)	Make someone understand something
Get away (from sth)	Type 3 (Transitive inseparable)	Leave in order to avoid something
Get away with (sth)	Type 4 (transitive inseparable with two prepositions)	Do something bad and not be punished or scolded for it
Get down to (sth)	Type 4 (Transitive inseparable with two prepositions)	Start doing something (working, studying, doing a project, etc.)
Get on/along (with sb)	Type 3 (Transitive inseparable)	Have a good relationship with a person
Get over (sth)	Type 3 (Transitive inseparable)	Overcome something (a sickness, a difficulty, etc.)
Get rid of (sth)	Type 4 (Transitive inseparable with two prepositions)	Dispose of something, no longer have it
Get through	Type 3 (Transitive inseparable)	Pass through something

Phrasal verb	Type	Meaning
Get through to (sb)	Type 4 (Transitive inseparable with two prepositions)	Contact someone
Call in	Type 1 (Intransitive inseparable)	Call a place, especially the place where you work, to inform them about something (sickness, delay, etc.)
Come down on (sb)	Type 4 (Transitive inseparable with two prepositions)	Rebuke someone very harshly
Go through (sth)	Type 3 (Transitive inseparable)	Have problems (or a difficult period)
Help (sb) out	Type 2 (Transitive separable)	Help someone
Talk (sb) out (of sth)	Type 2 (Transitive separable)	Try and convince someone that they are not making the right choice

Idiom/ Phrase/Collocation/ etc.	Meaning
A bright young thing (idiom)	Young and enthusiastic
A storm is brewing (idiom)	Trouble or a negative situation is about to happen or developing with potential negative consequences
A tempest in a teapot (AmE)/ A storm in a teapot (BrE) (idiom)	A big deal over nothing/ Excessive excitement over nothing
Be in (phrase)	Accept to be part of a project
Heavy-hearted (collocation)	Quite sad and thoughtful
Join forces (collocation)	Gather together to achieve a common goal
Make one's blood boil (idiom)	Make someone feel furious and indignant over something
Not believe one's ears (idiom)	Be extremely surprised
Pass with flying colors (idiom)	Pass an exam/ test with a very high score
See eye to eye (with sb) (idiom)	Entirely agree with someone
Storm at sb (idiom)	Address someone very angrily and aggressively

CHAPTER 8 - GO A PASSION FOR HORSES

Phrasal verb	Type	Meaning
Go after (sb)	Type 3 (Transitive inseparable)	Chase someone, follow someone
Go back	Type 1 (Intransitive inseparable)	Return
Go back on (sth)	Type 4 (Transitive inseparable with two prepositions)	Change one's mind
Go down	Type 1 (Intransitive inseparable)	Decrease, diminish
Go in for (sth)	Type 4 (Transitive inseparable with two prepositions)	Undertake something: 1) do an examination or take part in a competition; 2) choose something as a job
Go off	Type 1 (Intransitive inseparable)	1) Explode; 2) Ring (in case of an alarm or an alarm clock)
Go on	Type 1 (Intransitive inseparable)	Continue
Go on at (sb) (BrE)	Type 4 (Transitive inseparable with two prepositions)	Repeatedly criticize someone else
Go out of (a place)	Type 4 (Transitive inseparable with two prepositions)	Exit (a place)
Go over (sth)	Type 3 (Transitive inseparable)	Examine something
Take up (sth)	Type 2 (Transitive separable)	Pursue a new hobby or interest

Idiom/ Phrase/ Collocation/ etc.	Meaning
A glimmer of hope (collocation)	A small sign of improvement
Cross the line (idiom)	Exaggerate
Face the music (idiom)	Deal with the consequences of a choice
Go off the beaten path (idiom)	Step out of the conventional way of doing things
Put sb in a tough spot (idiom)	Put someone in a difficult situation

CHAPTER 9 - HAND/ KEEP - PUT YOUR THINKING CAP ON!

Phrasal verb	Type	Meaning
Hand (sth) in	Type 2 (Transitive separable)	Give something to an authority (teacher, police, etc.)
Hand (sth) out	Type 2 (Transitive separable)	Distribute something by hand
Keep (sb) back (used in the passive form) (AmE)	Type 2 (Transitive separable)	(AmE) Be retained/ be held back
Keep (sth) down	Type 2 (Transitive separable)	Be quiet/ not be noisy
Keep (sth) in	Type 2 (Transitive separable)	Restrain oneself from expressing emotions, opinions, etc.
Keep off (sth)	Type 3 (Transitive inseparable)	Avoid something
Keep on (+ ing)	Type 3 (Transitive inseparable)	Continue doing something
Keep to (sth)	Type 3 (Transitive inseparable)	Follow the given rules, direction, etc.
Keep up with (sb/sth)	Type 4 (Transitive inseparable with two prepositions)	Keep pace with someone or something
Breathe (sth) in	Type 2 (Transitive separable)	Inhale air
Breathe (sth) out	Type 2 (Transitive separable)	Exhale air
Carry (sth) off	Type 2 (Transitive separable)	Succeed in doing something difficult; execute, complete something perceived as difficult
Fall behind with (sth)	Type 4 (Transitive inseparable with two prepositions)	Fail to meet deadlines
Turn out	Type 1 (Intransitive inseparable)	Happen unexpectedly, revealing something unexpected

Idiom/ Phrase/ Collocation/ etc.	Meaning
Ace a test/ job interview (idiom)	Pass a test with a high score/ a job interview successfully
Cut the air with a knife (idiom)	Tension that can be tangibly felt in the air
Feel on edge (idiom)	Feel extremely nervous

Idiom/ Phrase/ Collocation/ etc.	Meaning
Get started (phrase)	Start, begin
Nail something (idiom)	Go very well, complete something successfully
Put on one's thinking cap (idiom)	Think about something seriously, with a focused mind
Race against time (idiom)	Not have enough time to achieve one's goal
Run things like clockwork (idiom)	Manage things in a timely, and well-organized manner
The cherry on top (AmE)/ The cherry on top of the cake (BrE) (idiom)	Some extra bonus added to an already good situation (like the cherry on top of a cake)
Well up with tears (idiom)	Eyes starting to fill with tears

CHAPTER 10 - LOOK - 3000

Phrasal verb	Type	Meaning
Look back on (sth)	Type 4 (Transitive inseparable with two prepositions)	Remember about some event in the past
Look down on (sb/sth)	Type 4 (Transitive inseparable with two prepositions)	Treat (or think of) someone or something poorly, showing superiority
Look forward to (sth)	Type 4 (Transitive inseparable with two prepositions)	Wait in anticipation
Look on (sb/sth)	Type 3 (Transitive inseparable)	Regard someone or something as a good example, etc.
Look out	Type 1 (Intransitive inseparable)	Beware of something
Look out for (sth)	Type 4 (Transitive inseparable with two prepositions)	Pay close attention to something specific
Look (sth) over	Type 2 (Transitive separable)	Examine something quickly
Look through (sth)	Type 3 (Transitive inseparable)	Search

Phrasal verb	Type	Meaning
Blow (sth) up	Type 2 (Transitive separable)	Explode
Figure (sth) out	Type 2 (Transitive separable)	Understand
Go down	Type 1 (Intransitive inseparable)	Decrease
Jump in	Type 1 (Intransitive inseparable)	Take action enthusiastically (often without thinking enough)
Pass by/ Go by	Type 1 (Intransitive inseparable)	Elapse
Phase in	Type 1 (Intransitive inseparable)	Introduce oneself or something into a new phase gradually

Idiom/ Phrase/ Collocation/ etc.	Meaning
Be at a turning point (phrase)	A time of decisive change
Be at stake (idiom)	Be liable to be lost, at risk, in danger
Be in a tight spot (idiom)	Be in a difficult position
Be the salt of the earth (idiom)	Be a good and honest person
Be torn (idiom)	Be undecided (between two things)
Catch one's eye (idiom)	Catch someone's attention
Green with envy (idiom)	Be envious
It's a piece of cake (idiom)	It's easy
Tender age (collocation)	In younger years of one's life
Train of thought (phrase)	A series of thoughts happening in one's mind
Weigh the pros and cons (phrase)	Ponder all the positive and negative aspects of a problem/ situation/ decision

CHAPTER 11 - MAKE - A TRIP DOWN MEMORY LANE

Phrasal Verb	Type	Meaning
(Be) Made up of (sth)	Type 4 (Transitive inseparable with two prepositions)	Be composed of
Make for (sth)	Type 3 (Transitive inseparable)	Go into a specific direction
Make of (sth)	Type 3 (Transitive inseparable)	Form an idea about something
Make (sb/sth) out	Type 2 (Transitive separable)	Understand someone or something
Make (sth) up (1)	Type 2 (Transitive separable)	Invent an excuse
Make (sth) up (2)	Type 2 (Transitive separable)	Create something
Make (sth) up (to sb)	Type 2 (Transitive separable)	Compensate for something perceived as lacking towards someone
Make up for (sth)	Type 4 (Transitive inseparable with two prepositions)	Compensate for something perceived as lacking
Make up with (sth/sb)	Type 4 (Transitive inseparable with two prepositions)	Make peace with someone
Cheer (sb) up	Type 2 (Transitive separable)	Try and make someone happy again
Cool (sth/sb) off	Type 2 (Transitive separable)	Refresh oneself or something after great heat
Pass away	Type 1 (Intransitive inseparable)	Die
Pass out	Type 1 (Intransitive inseparable)	Faint
Save (sth) up	Type 2 (Transitive separable)	Set money aside for something

Idiom/ Phrase/ Collocation/ etc.	Meaning
Act weird (phrase)	Behave differently than usual
A trip/walk down memory lane (idiom)	Time spent recollecting past memories
Be as good as new (idiom)	Be in very good condition

Idiom/ Phrase/ Collocation/ etc.	Meaning
Be at the wheel (idiom)	Drive
Be on cloud nine (idiom)	Be elated, extremely happy
Crack jokes (idiom)	Tell jokes
Feel blue (idiom)	Feel sad
Have the time of one's life (idiom)	Have lots of fun
Have a rush of memories (phrase)	A sudden and powerful recollection of memories
Memories came flooding back (phrase)	Memories came suddenly back
Not put much thought into something (phrase)	Not pay much attention to something
Out of the blue (idiom)	All of a sudden
Roar with laughter (collocation)	Laugh heartily, often loudly
Take it easy (idiom)	Relax

CHAPTER 12 - PUT - A BUMPY RIDE

Phrasal Verb	Type	Meaning
Put (sth) back/off	Type 2 (Transitive separable)	Postpone
Put (sb) down	Type 2 (Transitive separable)	Belittle someone, make them feel unimportant
Put (sth) down to	Type 4 (Transitive inseparable with two prepositions)	Attribute the cause to something
Put (sth) forward	Type 2 (Transitive separable)	Move (an event) to an earlier date or time
Put (sb) off	Type 2 (Transitive separable)	Demoralize
Put (sth) on (1)	Type 2 (Transitive separable)	Wear some items of clothing

Phrasal Verb	Type	Meaning
Put (sth) on (2)	Type 2 (Transitive separable)	Turn the lights on
Put (sth) out (1)	Type 2 (Transitive separable)	Turn the lights off
Put (sth) out (2)	Type 2 (Transitive separable)	Extinguish a source of fire
Put (sb) through to	Type 4 (Transitive inseparable with two prepositions)	Connect someone on the phone to someone else
Put (sb) up	Type 2 (Transitive separable)	Host someone
Put (sth) up	Type 2 (Transitive separable)	Build
Put up with (sth)	Type 4 (Transitive inseparable with two prepositions)	Tolerate, bear something unpleasant
Burn (sth) out	Type 2 (Transitive separable)	Cease to burn (spontaneously)
Call (sb) up	Type 2 (Transitive separable)	Call someone on the phone
Pay (sth) off	Type 2 (Transitive separable)	Pay a debt/ mortgage etc. in full
Turn on	Type 2 (Transitive separable)	Start a source of electricity so that it works
Turn off	Type 2 (Transitive separable)	Stop a source of electricity from working
Turn out	Type 1 (Intransitive inseparable)	Happen unexpectedly, revealing something unexpected

Idiom/ Phrase/ Collocation/ etc.	Meaning
A blessing in disguise (idiom)	Something positive after seeming negative
A bumpy ride (idiom)	A hard time
A once-in-a-lifetime opportunity (collocation)	A very special opportunity
A tough nut to crack (idiom)	Tough, difficult to deal with
Be on top of the world (idiom)	Be thrilled/ extremely happy

Idiom/ Phrase/ Collocation/ etc.	Meaning
Catch one's breath (idiom)	Rest a bit
Go the extra mile (idiom)	Exceed one's expectations, make an effort
Grin and bear it (idiom)	Resist, endure the difficulties without complaining, stoically
Lend a sympathetic ear (idiom)	Listen with sympathy
Open a can of worms (idiom)	Find a lot of problems
Pay off the effort (idiom)	Meet someone's efforts with a successful outcome
Smooth sailing (idiom)	Easy
The end is in sight (phrase)	The end is near

CHAPTER 13 - RUN/ SET - THE SALT OF THE EARTH

Phrasal verb	Type	Meaning
Run after (sb/sth)	Type 3 (Transitive inseparable)	Persistently pursue something or someone
Run (sth) by (sb)	Type 2 (Transitive separable)	Tell your ideas to someone (to ask for their opinion)
Run into (sb)	Type 3 (Transitive inseparable)	Meet someone by chance
Run into (sth)	Type 3 (Transitive inseparable)	Experience something generally perceived as difficult
Run out of (sth)	Type 4 (Transitive inseparable with two prepositions)	Finish one's supply of something
Run over (sth)	Type 3 (Transitive inseparable)	Quickly read, revise something
Run (sb/sth) over	Type 2 (Transitive separable)	Hit someone or something with a vehicle
Set about (sth)	Type 3 (Transitive inseparable)	Start doing something/ dealing with something

Phrasal verb	Type	Meaning
Set (sb) apart (from sth)	Type 2 (Transitive separable)	Be different from the rest (people, products, etc.)
Set (sth/sb) back	Type 2 (Transitive separable)	Delay (v.)
Set (sth) off	Type 2 (Transitive separable)	Have something explode
Set (sth) up	Type 2 (Transitive separable)	Establish, start, found
Set (sth) out	Type 2 (Transitive separable)	Write down something clearly and in a detailed way
Set out/ off	Type 1 (Intransitive inseparable)	Leave

Idiom/ Phrase/ Collocation/ etc.	Meaning
Be a good egg (idiom)	Be a good person
Be a smart cookie (idiom)	Be intelligent
Be down to earth (idiom)	Be practical, unpretentious
Be green with envy (idiom)	Be envious
Be/ Get on in years (idiom)	Be not so young any more
Be the apple of one's eye (idiom)	Be someone's favorite
Be the salt of the earth (idiom)	Be a fine and noble person
Have an ace up one's sleeve (idiom)	Have a secret resource
Have a vivid imagination (collocation)	Be imaginative

CHAPTER 14 - TAKE - TWO PEAS IN A POD

Phrasal verb	Type	Meaning
Take after (sb)	Type 3 (Transitive inseparable)	Resemble someone
Take (sth) back (1)	Type 2 (Transitive separable)	Admit that one is wrong about something
Take (sth) back (2)	Type 2 (Transitive separable)	Return an item
Take (sb) back (to the past)	Type 2 (Transitive separable)	Have someone remember things from the past
Take (sb) in	Type 2 (Transitive separable)	Take someone to live with you
Take off (1)	Type 1 (Intransitive inseparable)	Leave ground (airplane)
Take off (2)	Type 1 (Intransitive inseparable)	Improve one's situation
Take (days) off	Type 2 (Transitive separable)	Take a vacation
Take (sb) on	Type 2 (Transitive separable)	Hire someone; recruit someone
Take (sth) on	Type 2 (Transitive separable)	Accept a job or a responsibility
Take (sb) out	Type 2 (Transitive separable)	Invite someone to go out together
Take to (sb/sth)	Type 3 (Transitive inseparable)	Start liking someone or something
Take up (sth)	Type 3 (Transitive inseparable)	Start a new hobby or interest
Carry on	Type 1 (Intransitive inseparable)	Continue
Find (sth) out	Type 2 (Transitive separable)	Discover
Grow apart	Type 1 (Intransitive inseparable)	Stop being friends, become less close in a relationship
Grow up	Type 1 (Intransitive inseparable)	Become older/ become an adult
Pass away	Type 1 (Intransitive inseparable)	Die
Set off/out	Type 1 (Intransitive inseparable)	Leave

Phrasal verb	Type	Meaning
Try (sth) on	Type 2 (Transitive separable)	Put some clothes on to see if they fit
Turn out	Type 1 (Intransitive inseparable)	Reveal itself to be (good, bad, etc.)

Idiom/ Phrase/Collocation/ etc.	Meaning
At an early age (phrase)	When someone was very young
Be at fault (phrase)	Make a mistake
Be like two peas in a pod (idiom)	Extremely similar
Be/Keep in touch (phrase)	Communicate by phone, e-mail, etc.
Bear a striking resemblance to (sb) (phrase)	Look very similar
Blood is thicker than water (proverb)	Family bonds are extremely strong
Have butterflies in one's stomach (idiom)	Be very nervous or excited
Immediate family (collocation)	Close family members
Not be growing any younger (phrase)	Get old
Run a business/ company (collocation)	Manage a business/company, etc.
Take a leap of faith (idiom)	Make a decision despite all the uncertainties of the case
Take a walk/trip down memory lane (idiom)	Remember things from the past
Unbeknownst to (sb) (phrase)	Without someone knowing something

CHAPTER 15 - TURN - A DOG'S LIFE

Phrasal verb	Type	Meaning
Turn around	Type 1 (Intransitive inseparable)	Turn oneself in the opposite direction
Turn (sb) away	Type 2 (Transitive separable)	Refuse someone admittance to a place
Turn (sb/sth) down	Type 2 (Transitive separable)	Refuse something, like an invitation, or someone
Turn into (sth)	Type 3 (Transitive inseparable)	Transform into something else
Turn (sth) on	Type 2 (Transitive separable)	Switch something on
Turn (sth) off	Type 2 (Transitive separable)	Switch something off
Turn (sb) off	Type 2 (Transitive separable)	Make someone lose interest in something
Turn out	Type 1 (Intransitive inseparable)	Reveal itself, happen
Turn to (sb)	Type 3 (Transitive inseparable)	Ask someone for help and assistance
Turn up	Type 1 (Intransitive inseparable)	Arrive unexpectedly
Call in on (sb)	Type 3 (Transitive inseparable)	Pay a short visit
Come across (sth/sb)	Type 3 (Transitive inseparable)	Find/meet something/someone by chance
Cut (sth) up	Type 2 (Transitive separable)	Cut something in little pieces
End up	Type 1 (Intransitive inseparable)	Ultimately find oneself doing something
Figure (sth) out	Type 2 (Transitive separable)	Understand something
Pour (sth) in	Type 2 (Transitive separable)	Put some liquid into a container
Sort (sth) out	Type 2 (Transitive separable)	Solve a problem

Idiom/ Phrase/Collocation/ etc.	Meaning
A dog's life (idiom)	An unhappy existence full of difficulties
A scaredy cat (idiom)	A timid creature, easily scared by everything (used also for people)
In one piece (idiom)	Safe, unharmed
It's water under the bridge (idiom)	It's not important any more, especially after a quarrel, it means it's all forgotten
Pitch dark (collocation)	Completely dark
With a heavy heart (collocation)	Full of sadness

DEFINITIONS OF TERMS

Definition of Phrase:

1) (Grammar) A group of words that is part of, rather than the whole of, a sentence

2) (Expression) A short group of words that are often used together and have a particular meaning

Online Cambridge Dictionary

Definition of Collocation:

A combination of lexical words which frequently co-occur in texts: ex. Little baby; small amount; make a mistake.

Longman, Student Grammar of Spoken and Written English, Douglas Biber, Susan Conrad, Geoffrey Leech

Definition of Idiom:

A fixed expression with a meaning that cannot be determined from the individual parts: ex. kick the bucket.

Longman, Student Grammar of Spoken and Written English, Douglas Biber, Susan Conrad, Geoffrey Leech

The precise definition of every phrase (ex. Phrasal verb, idiom, collocation, phrase) presented in the book has been retrieved on the Online Cambridge Dictionary

APPENDIX: AMERICAN ENGLISH VS. BRITISH ENGLISH

SPELLING VARIATIONS

American English	British English
Center (n.)	Centre (n.)
Criticize (v.)	Criticise (v.)
Favorite (adj.)	Favourite (adj.)
Inquire (v.)	Enquire (v.)
Learned (past simple/past participle)	Learnt (past simple/past participle)
Mom (n.)	Mum (n.)
Neighbor (n.)	Neighbour (n.)
Pajamas (n.)	Pyjamas (n.)
Theater (n.)	Theatre (n.)
Tire (n.)	Tyre (n.)

VOCABULARY

American English	British English
College	University
Downtown	City centre
Driver license	Driving license
Duplex	Semi-detached house
Highway/ Freeway	Motorway

American English	British English
Kids (Informal)/ Children	Children
Movie theater	Cinema
Newsstand	Newsagent's
Soccer	Football
Store	Shop
Stove	Cooker
Sweater	Jumper
Truck	Lorry
Resume	CV
Vacation	Holiday
Yard	Garden

IDIOMS AND VERBS

American English	British English
A tempest in a teapot	A storm in a teacup
Be as healthy as an ox	Be as healthy as a horse
Call someone on the phone	Phone someone/ Call someone on the phone
The cherry on top	The cherry on top of the cake

SPECIAL THANKS

A heartfelt thank you to my husband, T. Mallinson, who helped me in the endless proof-reading process, kindly lent his voice to the Text n. 1 of every chapter, and gave me his invaluable, unconditional support in carrying out this ambitious project.

My gratitude also goes to all my students, in particular LT68, and GB for testing out this method, providing precious feedback, and encouraging me to continue on.

A big thank you to my own teachers:

A. De Salvio, my first English teacher, who made me love this wonderful language;

M. Battistella, who first mentioned the idea of writing a book one day;

M. Lettera, who taught me voiceover techniques;

J. Recio Lebedev, who enhanced my writing skills;

J. Poulton, who contributed to the proof-reading of the stories, and assisted me with accent coaching.

Finally, I'd like to thank W. Burns for his technical assistance with the book design and publishing process. Punctual and precise, working with him has been a pleasure.

ABOUT THE AUTHOR

Daniela Casti has been teaching English for more than 15 years, first for private language schools in Italy and then as a freelance tutor both in Italy and in the USA, where she currently lives. She graduated in Foreign Languages and Literature (English and Russian) in 2004 at the University of Trieste (Italy). She earned her CELTA Certificate (Certificate in Teaching English to Speakers of Other Languages) from Cambridge in 2011. She gained her CPE Cambridge Certificate (Proficiency C2) in 2017. Her students' age has ranged from 10 to 70, allowing her to understand how to best adjust to a learner's needs, based both on their age, level and personality. She teaches general English, English for language tests (university, school, Cambridge tests), and English for work.

Her core values are respect, patience, and a positive and encouraging attitude.

Email: info.danielacasti.esl@gmail.com
Instagram profile: englishwithdaniela
Preply tutor: Daniela C. at https://preply.com/en/tutor/1766416

www.ingramcontent.com/pod-product-compliance
Lightning Source LLC
Chambersburg PA
CBHW062044090426
42740CB00016B/3010